RETURN to YOURSELF

THE MENTAL GAME *of* TENNIS *and* LIFE

RETURN TO YOURSELF:
The Mental Game of Tennis and Life

FIRST EDITION
March 2026

Published by Emil Vassilev

www.NorthernVaTennis.com
Facebook: @emiltennismethod | Instagram: @emiltennismethod

ISBN: 979-8-234-06799-9
Library of Congress Cataloging-in-Publication Data

Library of Congress Case
Vassilev, Emil
Return To Yourself: The Mental Game of Tennis and Life
Case Number: 1-15144986931 | March 2026

Category: Self-Help, Self-Improvement, Mindset, Sports, Tennis, Coaching, Training & Conditioning, Philosophy

Author: Emil Vassilev | Info@NorthernVATennis.com

Editor: Jaclyn Shultz | Jaclyn.AShultz@gmail.com

Cover Designer & Prepared for Publishing: EliJah Blyden Sr.| www.EliTheBookGuy.com

Text Formatting: Jahshua E. Blyden

Published in the United States of America

For the players who keep showing up.

For the ones who fight for one more ball,
one more breath,
one more moment of clarity.

For the ones who feel deeply, care deeply,
and grow through the messy parts.

For the ones who are brave enough to look inward
and are honest enough to keep going.

This book is for you.
And for the version of you that's still becoming.

DISCLAIMER

Limit of Liability/Disclaimer of Warranty:
While the publisher and author used their best efforts in preparing this book, they make no representations or warranties with respect to the accuracy or completeness of the contents of this book and specifically disclaim any implied warranties of merchantability or fitness for a particular purpose. No warranty may be created or extended by sales representatives or written sales materials. The advice and strategies contained herein may not be a suitable for your situation. You should consult with a professional where appropriate. Neither the publisher, the author, nor the graphic artist shall be liable for damages.

PREFACE

***

Whether you are a tennis player or just a fan of the game, or not even into tennis, I believe I can get you to see the remarkable similarities between the game of tennis and life in general. You see, life and tennis have so much in common that we can always relate to it. For example, part of the tennis rules includes the word "love." Seriously, "love!" Now, how many sports can you think of that include that word in their rules or scoring?

The inspiration behind my second book comes from my many years of coaching tennis and the different people I have met on and off the tennis court along the way. During my tennis lessons over the years, I have often tried to compare tennis to life because they are so very similar in many ways. One of the first things I do when I have a new client is to find out what their interests and hobbies are, what they do or used to do for a living, and what, if any, tennis goals they have. That helps me figure out how they think, how they process information, and how they approach new challenges. All those things are very important when trying to learn something new, like a sport or a language.

We all go through life facing many challenges, dealing with different situations and events. If you really think about it, what happens on the tennis court is very similar to what happens in life. It is a constant roller coaster of emotions. You have options: you can face the challenges presented to you head-on, or you can shy away. When you choose to directly face these challenges, you could also fail. The thing is, if you never face a challenge, you never learn anything. You see, in tennis, we as coaches often have players who have played in a certain way for a long, long time, but in order for that player to take their game to the next level, they have to choose between learning something new (which will suck for a while) or remaining the same. The choices you make determine the level of improvement that you can reach in anything in life.

I am extremely grateful to have been through many, many challenges in my life. I can honestly say that I am who I am today because of the challenges I faced head-on. Some I failed, but many I conquered. I am very grateful that I was put in those situations because otherwise, I never would have been able to unleash my full potential. One thing I tell all my junior players is, "Do not be afraid to F.A.I.L." To me, FAIL stands for First Attempt In Learning. So go ahead and fail as many times as needed, because eventually you will get it right, and that's when all the fun begins!

I truly hope that this book helps you become your absolute best on and off the tennis court. Take on those daily life challenges the same way you would if you were on the tennis court or vice versa. I wish you the best of luck on your journey to self-improvement.

– Coach Emil

CONTENTS

***

RETURN to YOURSELF

THE MENTAL GAME *of* TENNIS *and* LIFE

BY EMIL VASSILEV

INTRODUCTION

The Court of Life and Tennis

***

If you've spent enough time on a tennis court — whether as a player, coach, or even just a fan — you start to realize something: Tennis has a funny way of revealing who you are. Not the polished version you show the world, but the real you. The one who shows up under pressure, after mistakes, when the match isn't going your way.

For me, the serve has always been the clearest mirror. It's the one shot you control completely. No opponent, no rally, no chaos — just you, the ball, and whatever is going on in your head. And yet, despite all that control, the serve is also where things can unravel the fastest. One bad toss, one tight shoulder, one moment of hesitation ... and suddenly you're staring at a double fault, wondering how the hell you missed two chances in a row.

Over the years — as a player, as a coach, and as someone who's lived a life full of its own double faults — I've come to see the serve as more than a tennis stroke. It's a metaphor for the choices we make, the risks we take, and the way we respond when things don't go according to plan.

The Double Fault: When Life Misses Twice

A double fault in tennis is simple: two missed serves, point lost. But anyone who's ever played knows it's never just about the point. It's about the moment. The pressure. The doubt. The sudden awareness that you're not as in control as you thought.

Life works the same way.

Sometimes you make a mistake — your "first fault." Maybe it's a bad decision, a missed opportunity, or a conversation you wish you handled differently. And then, because you're human, you try to fix it too quickly. You rush. You tighten up. You overthink. And boom — the second mistake lands right on top of the first.

That's your double fault.

I've seen it in players. I've lived it myself. And if you're reading this, you've lived it, too.

Risk, Reward, and the Choices We Make

Every serve is a decision. Go big and risk missing or play it safe and give your opponent a look at the ball? Players wrestle with this every point, and honestly, so do we in life.

Do you take the job that scares you?

Do you end the relationship that's draining you?

Do you speak up when staying quiet feels easier?

Power is great, but without direction, it's just noise. Precision is what changes things. The same way a well-placed serve can open up the whole court, a well-aimed decision can open up your whole life.

The Mental Battle No One Sees

Here's the part most people don't talk about: Double faults aren't really about technique. They're about psychology. Confidence. Nerves. The stories you tell yourself between points.

I've coached players who could hit 20 perfect serves in a row during practice, then double-fault three times in a game because their mind got in the way. And I've been that player too — the one who knows exactly what to do, but can't get out of his own head long enough to do it.

Life is no different. Pressure exposes us. Mistakes shake us. But resilience — that ability to reset, breathe, and step up again — that's what separates the players who grow from the ones who spiral.

Consistency, Practice, and the Long Game

A reliable serve doesn't show up overnight. It's built through repetition, frustration, small adjustments, and a willingness to keep showing up even when it feels like you're not getting anywhere. Life rewards the same qualities. Every mistake is feedback. Every setback is a rep.

Every double fault is a chance to learn something about yourself.

Adaptability: The Hidden Skill

The best servers aren't stubborn — they're adaptable. They change their toss in the wind. They adjust their targets under pressure. They read the moment and respond.

Life demands the same flexibility. Plans change. People change. Circumstances shift. The ones who thrive aren't the strongest or the smartest — they're the ones who can pivot without losing themselves.

A New Way to See Your Mistakes

This book isn't about avoiding double faults — in tennis or in life. That's impossible. It's about understanding them. Learning from them and using them. Because every serve is a new beginning. Every point is a fresh chance. And every double fault is a reminder that perfection isn't the goal — growth is.

If you're ready, let's step up to the line together.

Before we can talk about how to fix double faults — in tennis or in life — we need to understand what they really are. Not just technically, but mentally and emotionally. Because a double fault isn't just two missed serves. It's a moment where pressure, doubt, and decision-making collide.

So let's break it down. Let's look at what a double fault actually represents — and why it shows up when it does.

PART I

THE SERVE —WHERE IT ALL BEGINS

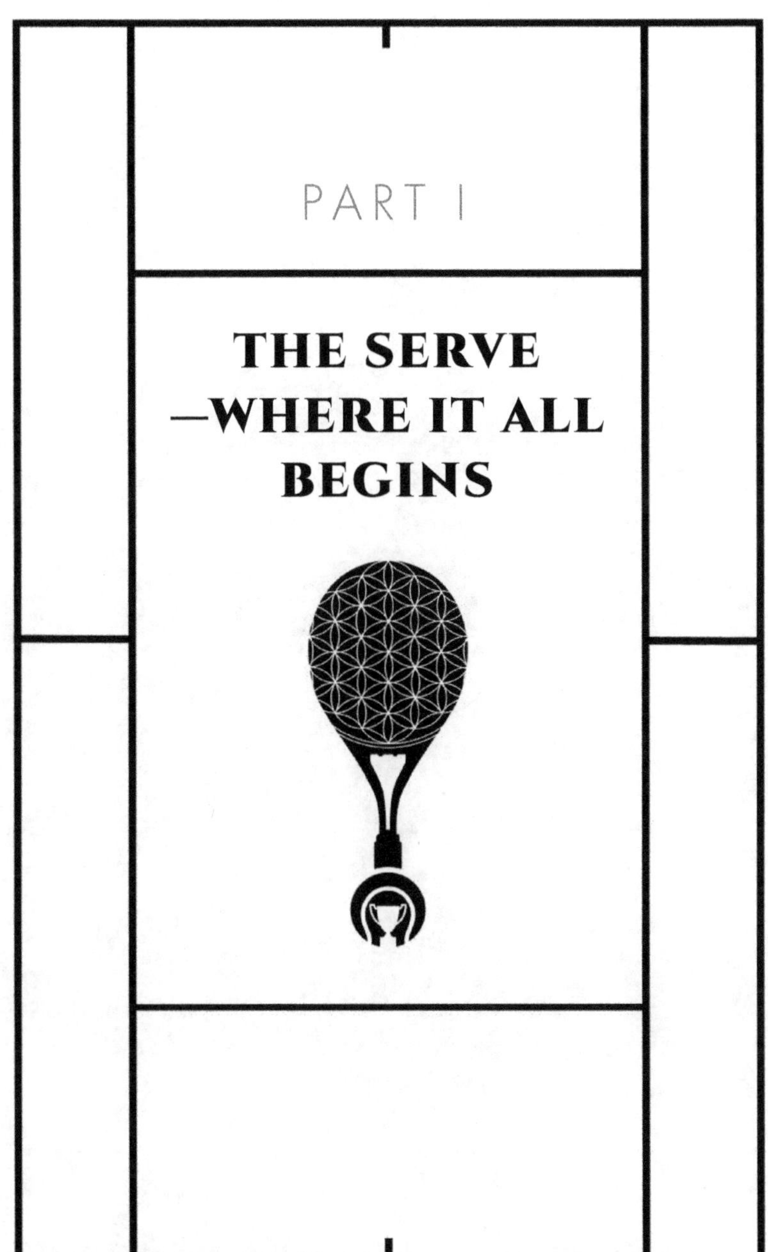

CHAPTER 1

Understanding the Double Fault

***

Tennis and Life's Dual Errors

If you've ever stood on a baseline with the ball in your hand and your heart in your throat, you know this truth: A double fault is never just a missed serve. It's a moment where your technique, your nerves, and your mindset collide. It exposes you a little. It humbles you a lot.

And the interesting thing is, life works the same way.

A double fault isn't just two bad swings — it's two decisions, two reactions, two moments where things didn't go the way you planned. I've seen players unravel after one. I've also seen people unravel after one, and I've been there myself, both on the court and off it. So let's try to break it down.

The Serve in Life

A serve is the only shot in tennis where you have complete control. No opponent dictating pace. No rally forcing you into defense. Just you, your preparation, and your intention.

Life gives us moments like that, too — the job you apply for, the relationship you start, the risk you take. Those are your first serves. You toss the ball up, hoping for an ace, or at least a clean start, but sometimes the ball doesn't land where you want it to.

The First Fault: When Plans Don't Go as Planned

The first fault is usually a surprise. You thought you had it. You thought you were ready. And then ... something's off.

In tennis, maybe your toss drifted. Maybe your legs didn't load. Maybe you rushed. In life, it's the same story:

- You miss out on the promotion you thought was yours.
- A conversation goes sideways.
- A project you poured yourself into falls flat.

The first fault stings, but it's manageable. It's a reminder to adjust, breathe, and reset. Next comes the real test.

The Double Fault: When Mistakes Start to Cluster

The second serve is where the pressure lives. Everyone watching knows it. You know it. Your body definitely knows it. And this is also where things can snowball.

In tennis, the fear of missing again tightens your arm. You guide the ball instead of hitting it. You play not to lose instead of playing to win.

In life, the same pattern shows up again and again. You make one mistake, and instead of slowing down, you speed up. You rush into the next project without thinking. You try to fix a misunderstanding by overcorrecting, and suddenly the situation is worse than when you started. You panic after one slip and create another. It's the same rhythm as a double fault — pressure meets fear, and the moment tightens around you. It's not technical, it's human.

Learning From the Double Fault

Most players — and most people — misunderstand what a double fault really is. They treat it like a verdict, a statement about who they are or what they're capable of. But a double fault isn't a sentence. It's feedback. It's information. It's the moment saying, "Hey, something's off. Let's look at it."

When a player double-faults, I always tell them the same thing: "That point is gone. You're still here."

This is a reminder that the mistake is already in the past, but you are still in the match. Life demands that same reset. One mistake doesn't define your story — unless you let it.

Sometimes the adjustment is small. In tennis, it might be slowing down your toss, changing your target, or loosening your grip. In life, it might be speaking a little more clearly, planning instead of reacting, or letting yourself ask for help instead of trying to muscle through everything alone. Tiny shifts can prevent big spirals.

And then there's pressure — the thing we all try to avoid but can never escape. Pressure isn't the enemy. Panic is. The players who handle pressure well aren't fearless; they've just learned to breathe through the moment instead of fighting it. They've learned to stay with themselves when things get loud. Life works the same way. Pressure is simply a sign that something matters.

When the mistake happens — when the double fault lands — the best players don't hide from it. They acknowledge it, adjust, and keep swinging. Accountability is a kind of superpower. It turns mistakes into momentum.

The Bigger Lesson

A double fault teaches you more than a clean ace ever will. It shows you where your mind goes under stress. It shows you how you react when things slip. It shows you whether you trust yourself enough to keep going.

In tennis and in life, the goal isn't perfection. It's resilience. It's awareness. It's the ability to step up to the line again after missing twice and still believe in your swing.

Because the match isn't decided by the faults — it's decided by what you do next.

The Psychology of Mistakes

If you've ever double-faulted at a bad moment — and every player has — you know it's rarely about the mechanics. The technique might look off, but the real breakdown happens in the space between your ears. A double fault is a psychological event wearing the mask of a technical error. Life works the same way. We don't mess up because we don't know what to do. We mess up because pressure, fear, and doubt get loud enough to drown out what we already know.

When the Moment Feels Too Big

I've coached players who could hit fifty perfect serves in practice, then walk into a match and miss two in a row because their hand suddenly felt foreign. That's nerves. That's pressure. That's the mind hijacking the body.

In life, the same thing happens. You stumble through an interview you prepared for. You freeze during a presentation. You say something you don't mean because anxiety squeezes your voice. You make a rushed decision because you feel cornered.

But remember: "Pressure doesn't create new weaknesses — it exposes the ones already there."

When You Think Too Much

"Overthinking is the enemy of execution."

One of the worst things a player can do before a serve is think too much. The serve is rhythm, timing, and flow. But when you start analyzing every tiny movement — your toss, your elbow, your wrist — you disconnect from the natural motion. You become mechanical. And mechanical players double-fault. Life mirrors this perfectly. Overthinking leads to hesitation, second-guessing, and paralysis. You talk yourself out of opportunities you're ready for. You shrink from moments you're capable of handling.

When Confidence Slips

"A double fault is often just a moment where belief wavers."

Confidence is invisible until it disappears. A player who loses confidence starts guiding the ball instead of hitting it. They aim instead of swinging. They play small. They play scared.

In life, confidence slips after rejection, failure, criticism, or a moment where you didn't show up the way you hoped. And once confidence dips, mistakes multiply — not because you're incapable, but because you stop trusting yourself.

The Parallels Are Everywhere

A player who panics after a first fault rushes the second serve. A person who panics after a mistake rushes the next decision. Overthinking a serve leads to a miss. Overthinking a conversation leads to silence or awkwardness. Test anxiety can make a smart student fail. Match anxiety can make a great server crumble. The psychology is the same — only the setting changes.

Breaking the Cycle

The good news is this: The mind can be trained just like the body. Players rehearse their serve mentally — you can rehearse your success in stressful moments. A deep breath before a serve resets the system — a deep breath before a big moment in life does the same. A pre-serve routine calms the mind — a personal routine before meetings, conversations, or decisions does too. And the way you talk to yourself matters. Players who spiral after a fault talk to themselves like critics. Players who recover talk to themselves like coaches. A double fault isn't a character flaw. It's data. It's feedback. It's a chance to adjust. Life's mistakes work the same way.

The Real Lesson

Double faults — in tennis or in life — aren't signs that you're failing. They're signs that you're human. They reveal where your mind goes under pressure. They reveal how you respond to fear. They reveal the stories you tell yourself when things slip. And once you understand the psychology behind your mistakes, you can change the pattern instead of repeating it. The goal isn't to eliminate mistakes. It's to stop letting them control you.

Now that we've unpacked the mechanics and psychology behind double faults, it's time to look at how the best players in the world handle them. Because the truth is, even the legends crack under pressure. Even the champions double-fault. Even the icons lose their way for a moment. The difference is how they respond. So let's study the greats — not to idolize them, but to learn from the way they recover, reset, and rise.

CHAPTER 2

LEARNING FROM THE GREATS

***

RESILIENCE AND MENTAL RECOVERY IN TENNIS

One of the things I've always loved about tennis is that even the legends — the players we put on pedestals — crack under pressure sometimes. They double-fault. They lose their cool. They make decisions they regret. And yet, they find ways to recover that most people never see. When you study the greats, you realize something important: Their greatness isn't built on perfection — it's built on how they respond when perfection breaks down.

Let's look at two moments from Serena Williams and Roger Federer that show exactly what I mean.

CASE STUDY 1: SERENA WILLIAMS — THE 2018 US OPEN FINAL

The Moment

If you watched that final against Naomi Osaka, you remember the tension. Serena wasn't just playing for a title — she was chasing history. The match got emotional, heated, and complicated. And in the middle of all that chaos, she double-faulted at a brutal moment. Now, a double fault in a Grand Slam final is one thing. A double fault in a Grand Slam final while the entire stadium is buzzing with controversy is something else entirely.

What Serena Teaches Us:

1. **Emotional Control Isn't About Being Calm — It's About Staying Present**

   Serena didn't fold. She didn't walk off. She kept competing. That alone is a lesson.

   In life, you don't need to be emotionless — you just need to stay in the moment long enough to make your next move.

2. **Turning Pain into Purpose**

   After the match, Serena didn't hide from what happened. She used it to talk about fairness, respect, and gender equality in sports. That's a powerful reminder: Sometimes your worst moments become the platform for your strongest message.

3. **Growth Isn't Always Technical**

   Serena didn't walk away thinking, "I need to fix my serve." She walked away thinking about how she wanted to handle pressure, conflict, and emotion moving forward. That's the kind of growth that lasts.

Case Study 2: Roger Federer — The 2008 Wimbledon Final

The Moment

If you ask tennis fans about the greatest match ever played, most will point to Federer vs. Nadal in the 2008 Wimbledon final. It was a war. A masterpiece. A match where both players were pushed to their absolute limits. And in the fifth set tiebreak — with the entire world watching — Federer double-faulted. Not exactly the moment you want to blink.

What Federer Teaches Us:

1. **Grace Under Pressure Isn't a Personality Trait — It's a Skill**

Federer didn't panic. He didn't spiral. He didn't let the double fault define the rest of the match. He simply moved on to the next point. That's a skill anyone can train: the ability to reset instantly.

2. **Immediate Recovery Matters More Than the Mistake**

Federer fought back after that double fault. He didn't win the match, but he didn't collapse either.

In life, the mistake isn't what hurts you — it's the reaction that follows.

3. **Long-Term Resilience Is Built Through Losses**

Federer has talked openly about how that match shaped him. Losses like that don't break champions — they build them. And the same is true for anyone willing to learn from their setbacks.

Extracted Lessons From the Greats

1. **Even the Best Make Mistakes**

Serena. Federer. Nadal. Djokovic.
They all double-fault.
They all crack under pressure.
If they can accept imperfection, so can we.

2. **Resilience Is the Real Separator**

The greats aren't great because they avoid mistakes. They're great because they recover faster than everyone else.

3. Mental Recovery Techniques Work — On and Off the Court

Breathing. Positive self-talk. Reset routines. These aren't clichés — they're tools the best athletes in the world rely on.

4. Setbacks Can Become Fuel

Serena turned controversy into advocacy.
Federer turned heartbreak into evolution.
You can turn your double faults into something meaningful, too.

5. Reflection Is a Superpower

Champions don't just move on — they look back with honesty. Not to judge themselves, but to understand themselves.

6. How You Handle Failure Shapes Your Legacy

People remember how you respond. Grace, humility, accountability — these qualities outlast trophies.

Life Lessons From the Legends

Elite athletes live under pressure that most people never experience. But the way they handle it gives us a blueprint for our own lives:

1. Embrace Pressure

Pressure means you're in the arena.
It means something matters.

2. Focus on the Next Point

Federer mastered this.
You can too.

3. **Build Routines That Ground You**
   Djokovic does it before every serve.
   You can do it before every challenge.

4. **Learn From Losses**
   Nadal built a career on turning setbacks into fuel.

5. **Take Care of Your Mind**
   Simone Biles showed the world that mental health is part of performance.

6. **Lose With Grace**
   Phelps taught us that honesty about struggle is strength, not weakness.

7. **Never Count Yourself Out**
   Tiger Woods proved that comebacks are always possible.

8. **Lean on Your Support System**
   Even Usain Bolt needed a team behind him.

The Real Takeaway

The greats aren't superhuman. They're human beings who learned how to navigate pressure, mistakes, and expectations better than most. And the truth is, you don't need to be a Grand Slam champion to apply their lessons. You just need to be willing to look at your own double faults — in tennis and in life — and decide they're not the end of your story.

Learning from champions is powerful — but inspiration alone doesn't change your serve or your life. At some point, you need tools. You need techniques. You need habits you can actually practice. So now we shift from theory to application.

From stories to skills. From watching the greats to becoming more consistent yourself.

Let's break down the techniques that reduce double faults — and the habits that make your serve something you can trust under pressure.

CHAPTER 3

Techniques to Minimize Double Faults

***

Mastering the Serve — and Yourself

If you've coached or played long enough, you start to realize something: Most double faults don't come from a broken serve — they come from a broken moment. A moment where your mind, your body, and your intention aren't aligned. But here's the good news: The serve is one of the most trainable shots in tennis. And when you understand the fundamentals — the *real* fundamentals — you can dramatically reduce double faults without reinventing your entire motion.

These are the same principles I've taught juniors, adults, college players, and even players who walked onto the court terrified of serving. They work because they're simple, repeatable, and grounded in reality.

Let's break them down.

1. Perfecting the Toss

The serve starts before the swing. If your toss is inconsistent, everything else becomes guesswork. I've seen players with beautiful mechanics fall apart because their toss wanders like a lost balloon.

What matters most:

- Consistency: Your toss should land in the same spot every time — slightly in front, slightly to the right (if you're right-handed), and high enough to give you time to load.
- Relaxation: A tense toss arm creates chaos. Let the ball roll off your fingertips instead of "throwing" it.

Drills I give players:

- Stationary Toss Drill: Toss and catch without swinging. If you can't catch it comfortably at its peak, your toss isn't consistent yet.
- Eyes-Closed Toss: Sounds strange, but it forces you to feel the motion instead of micromanaging it visually.

"A good toss doesn't guarantee a good serve — but a bad toss guarantees a bad one."

2. Grip Adjustment

Your grip is your connection to the ball. If you're not using a continental grip, you're basically trying to build a house with the wrong tools. The continental grip gives you versatility, spin, and control — everything you need to avoid double faults.

What I tell players:

- Hold the racket like you're shaking hands with it
- Your knuckles should line up with the edge of the frame
- It should feel neutral, not forced

Why it matters:

A proper grip lets you:

- Hit flat serves
- Hit slice serves
- Hit kick serves
- Adjust under pressure

A bad grip forces you into predictable, stiff motions — and predictable, stiff motions break down under pressure.

3. Stance and Footwork

Your serve starts from the ground up. Players often obsess over their arm, but the serve is a full-body movement. Your stance sets the foundation.

Two main stances:

- Platform: Feet stay apart. More stability. Great for consistency.
- Pinpoint: Back foot slides up. More power. Less stability.

What matters most:

- Balance
- Rhythm
- A smooth weight transfer

If your stance feels rushed or unstable, your serve will follow.

Footwork drill:

Practice moving from your ready position into your serving stance with no ball. Smoothness matters more than speed.

4. The Serve Motion

This is where everything comes together. A great serve isn't about muscling the ball — it's about sequencing. When the body works in the right order, the serve feels effortless.

Key checkpoints:

- Racket Back: Start low and relaxed
- Trophy Position: Elbow up, racket pointing behind you or upward
- Contact Point: As high as you can comfortably reach
- Body Drive: Legs, hips, and shoulders generate power — not just your arm

Drills:

- Shadow Swings: No ball, just motion. Build the pattern.
- Half-Speed Serves: Slow everything down to feel the sequence.

If your motion feels rushed, your serve will be rushed. If your motion feels smooth, your serve will follow.

5. Follow-Through

Finish the serve — don't quit on it. A lot of double faults come from players stopping their motion early because they're nervous. The follow-through keeps your swing committed and your body balanced.

What to look for:

- Racket finishes across your body for flat serves
- Higher or more exaggerated finish for spin serves
- Your momentum should carry you forward naturally

A full follow-through is a sign of trust — trust in your motion, trust in your swing, trust in yourself.

6. Mental Preparation

The serve is 50% mechanics, 50% mindset. You can have perfect technique and still double-fault if your mind is racing.

Tools that work:

- Visualization: Picture the serve going in before you hit it
- Breathing: One deep breath can reset your entire system
- Routine: A consistent pre-serve routine calms the mind and anchors your focus

"Your routine is your anchor. Build one you can rely on."

7. Practice Under Pressure

If you only practice serves when you're relaxed, you're not practicing for reality. Double faults happen under pressure — so you need to train under pressure.

Pressure drills:

- Serve Games: You must make a certain number of serves to "win."
- Timed Serving: Set a timer and hit as many quality serves as you can.
- Consequence Serving: Miss two in a row? Reset the count.

Pressure isn't the enemy — unpreparedness is.

8. Video Analysis

The camera doesn't lie. Players often think they're doing one thing, but the video shows something completely different. Watching yourself serve is one of the fastest ways to improve.

What to look for:

- Toss height
- Balance
- Racket path
- Follow-through
- Timing

"Awareness is the first step toward mastery."

From the Court to Character

Reducing double faults isn't about perfection — it's about building a serve you can trust. A serve that holds up when the match gets tight. A serve that doesn't disappear when your nerves show up. A serve that reflects your preparation, not your panic. Every part of the serve — from the toss to the follow-through — is a chance to build reliability. And every double fault is a chance to learn something about your technique, your mindset, or your habits. The goal isn't to eliminate double faults entirely. The goal is to make them rare — and irrelevant.

Everything you just learned about the serve — the toss, the stance, the motion, the follow-through — applies to more than tennis. These aren't just physical skills. They're life skills disguised as technique.

So let's zoom out. Let's take the lessons from the court and translate them into the decisions, relationships, and challenges you face every day. Because the serve doesn't just teach you how to play better. It teaches you how to live better.

CHAPTER 4

LIFE TECHNIQUES

***

HOW TENNIS TEACHES YOU TO LIVE BETTER

One of the reasons I love tennis — and why I've spent so much of my life teaching it — is that the game doesn't stay on the court. The lessons follow you home. They show up in your relationships, your decisions, your career, and your confidence. And the more you understand the mechanics of the serve, the more you start to see how those same mechanics apply to the way you move through life. Let's take the techniques we just covered and translate them into something bigger — something you can use even when you're nowhere near a tennis court.

1. Perfecting the Toss → Strategic Planning

Consistency creates clarity.

A good toss sets up the entire serve. A bad toss forces you into survival mode. Life works the same way. When you plan with consistency — when your goals, habits, and intentions line up — everything becomes easier. You're not scrambling. You're not reacting. You're not guessing.

Life application:

- Build routines that support your goals
- Keep your priorities in front of you
- Don't "toss" your energy in random directions

"A consistent toss gives you a clean swing. A consistent plan gives you a clean life."

2. Grip Adjustment → Adaptability and Versatility

You can't use the same grip for every serve — or the same approach for every situation. In tennis, the continental grip gives you options. It lets you adjust. It gives you freedom.

In life, adaptability is your continental grip.

Life application:

- Some situations require power
- Some require finesse
- Some require patience
- Some require a completely different angle

"If you only know one way to respond, you'll struggle when life throws you something unexpected. Versatility is strength."

3. Stance and Footwork → Staying Grounded While Staying Mobile

You need a stable base — but you also need to move. A good stance gives you balance. Good footwork gives you options. You need both. Life demands the same combination.

Life application:

- Know your values — that's your platform stance.
- Be willing to pivot when life changes — that's your pinpoint stance.

Stability without movement makes you rigid. Movement without stability makes you chaotic. The sweet spot is both.

4. **The Serve Motion → Executing with Purpose**

Preparation, rhythm, and intention matter more than force.

A serve isn't just a swing — it's a sequence. When the sequence is right, the power shows up naturally. Life is no different.

Life application:

- Prepare before you act
- Engage your whole self — mind, body, emotion
- Move with intention, not impulse

When your actions line up with your purpose, life feels smoother — just like a clean service motion.

5. **Follow-Through → Commitment**

Don't quit on the motion — or on yourself. A lot of players miss serves because they stop their swing early. They get tight. They get scared. They try to "place" the ball instead of hitting it. People do the same thing in life.

Life application:

- Finish what you start
- Don't pull back just because you're nervous
- Trust the work you've put in

A full follow-through is a sign of belief — in your technique, your preparation, and your direction.

6. **Mental Preparation → Mindset and Visualization**

Your mind swings before your body does.

Players who visualize their serve perform better. Players who breathe before they hit perform better. Players who have a routine perform better. Life rewards the same habits.

Life application:

- Visualize the outcome you want
- Build routines that calm your mind
- Use breathing to reset your system

Your mindset is the first serve. Everything else follows.

7. Practice Under Pressure → Stress Training

"If you only train in comfort, you won't perform in chaos."

Players who never practice pressure situations crumble when the match gets tight. It's not because they're weak — it's because they're unprepared. Life is full of tiebreakers.

Life application:

- Put yourself in situations that stretch you
- Practice speaking up
- Practice making decisions
- Practice staying calm when things get loud

"Pressure becomes easier when you've met it before."

8. Video Analysis → Honest Self-Reflection

You can't fix what you refuse to see. Players are often shocked when they watch themselves serve. What they think they're doing and what they're actually doing are rarely the same. Life is no different.

Life application:

- Reflect on your choices.
- Look at your patterns.
- Be honest about your habits.

Self-awareness is the first step toward self-improvement.

The Bigger Picture

The serve teaches you how to live:

- Plan with consistency
- Adapt with confidence
- Stay grounded but flexible
- Execute with intention
- Commit fully
- Prepare mentally
- Train under pressure
- Reflect honestly

These aren't just tennis skills — they're life skills. And when you start applying them off the court, you'll notice something powerful: Your double faults in life start to disappear, too.

Once you start applying tennis principles to your life, you begin to see patterns — especially around how you make decisions. And one of the biggest patterns is this: Most mistakes come from force, not intention. Which brings us to one of the most important lessons in both tennis and life: *precision beats power.*

Let's break down why.

CHAPTER 5

PRECISION OVER POWER

***

THE ART OF THOUGHTFUL DECISION-MAKING

If you've ever watched a player try to blast their way out of trouble with a 120-mph second serve, you already know how this story ends. Power without purpose is chaos. It looks impressive for a second, but it rarely lands where it needs to. And honestly, life works the same way. We live in a world that glorifies "big moves," "big risks," and "big swings." But the truth — the truth every good server learns — is that precision beats power far more often than the other way around.

Let's break down what that really means.

POWER IS LOUD, PRECISION IS EFFECTIVE

In tennis, power gets the highlight reels. Aces. Huge serves. The kind that makes the crowd gasp.

But ask any coach or any seasoned player, and they'll tell you the same thing: The serve that wins matches isn't the fastest one — it's the one that lands where you want it to. Life is no different.

People chase big, dramatic actions:

- Quitting a job overnight
- Jumping into relationships too fast
- Making impulsive decisions because they "feel right" in the moment

But the decisions that actually move your life forward are usually the ones made with clarity, intention, and accuracy.

Precision is quiet, but it's powerful.

Precision Comes From Awareness, Not Force

A great serve isn't created by swinging harder — it's created by understanding:

- Your target
- Your timing
- Your rhythm
- Your intention

Life rewards the same awareness.

Precision in life looks like:

- Choosing your words carefully in a tough conversation
- Taking time to understand a situation before reacting
- Setting boundaries instead of exploding
- Making decisions based on values, not emotions

Power tries to dominate the moment. Precision tries to understand it.

Power Breaks Down Under Pressure While Precision Holds Up

When the score tightens, players who rely only on power start to crumble. Their margin for error disappears. Their confidence dips. Their swing tightens. But players who rely on precision? They stay steady. They stay composed. They trust their placement, not their muscle. Life works the same way. Precision — thoughtful, intentional action — is what holds up when things get real.

Precision Doesn't Mean Playing Small

This is important.

Precision isn't about being timid. It's not about avoiding risk. It's not about playing safe.

It's about aiming with purpose. A well-placed serve can be just as aggressive as a powerful one — sometimes more. It opens the court. It sets up the point. It puts you in control.

In life, precision means:

- Taking the right risks
- At the right time
- For the right reasons

How to Build Precision in Your Life

1. **Slow Down Before You Act**

   A rushed serve rarely lands.
   A rushed decision rarely helps.

2. **Know Your Target**

   In tennis, you don't just "hit the serve." You pick a spot.
   In life, pick a direction — not just a feeling.

3. **Remove the Extra Noise**

   Overthinking kills precision. So does emotional clutter. Clear your mind before you swing.

4. **Trust the Process**

   Precision comes from repetition. From practice. From showing up consistently.

Life rewards the same discipline.

The Real Lesson

Power is tempting. It feels good. It looks good. It gives you the illusion of control.

But precision — thoughtful, intentional, well-aimed action — is what actually changes things, on the court and off it. When you learn to value precision over power, you stop trying to force outcomes and start creating them. You stop swinging wildly and start hitting with purpose. You stop reacting and start choosing. And that's when everything begins to shift.

CHAPTER 6

Second Serves and Second Chances

***

Why Redemption Is Built Into the Game

If there's one thing I wish every player understood — and every person, honestly — it's this: Tennis gives you a second serve for a reason. The sport is literally designed to give you another chance after you miss. Not because you're supposed to be perfect, but because you're supposed to keep trying.

Life works the same way. It just doesn't always announce the second serve as clearly. But it's there. And learning to recognize it — and trust it — is one of the most powerful skills you can develop.

The Second Serve: A Built-In Reset Button

A good second serve never comes from fear. It comes from trust — trust in your mechanics, trust in your preparation, trust in your ability to stay composed when the margin for error shrinks. When you're standing on that baseline with one fault already behind you, the second serve becomes a small test of who you are in that moment. Not who you are when everything is flowing, but who you are when things tighten.

Life is full of those moments, too. The job you didn't get. The relationship that fell apart. The opportunity you weren't ready for. The mistake you made when emotions were louder than your judgment. Life rarely ends on the first fault. It almost always gives you another swing — if you're willing to take it.

The reason people fear the second serve is the same reason they fear second chances: They're terrified of failing again. The second serve exposes you. It reveals your nerves, your self-talk, your habits, and your resilience. It's the moment where your brain whispers, "Don't miss again." And that whisper can feel louder than any stadium.

But here's the truth I've seen over and over: Playing scared is the fastest way to double fault — in tennis and in life. When you try to avoid losing, you stop giving yourself a chance to win.

A second serve you can trust isn't built on fear or caution. It's built on clarity. It's built on having a version of your game that holds up when things get tight. In life, that means having a version of yourself that shows up when things get messy. It means building habits that don't fall apart when emotions spike. It means having routines that ground you when uncertainty hits. It means cultivating a mindset that doesn't collapse after one mistake.

A strong second serve is built through repetition. A strong second chance is built through reflection. Both require you to look honestly at what happened, learn from it, and step back up with intention.

There's something deeply human about the second serve. It's a moment of vulnerability, but also a moment of possibility. A second serve says, "You're allowed to try again." A second chance says, "You're allowed to grow." Redemption isn't about erasing the first mistake — it's about proving to yourself that the mistake doesn't define you.

I've coached players who were terrified of missing twice. They'd guide the ball, push it, baby it over the net. And ironically, that fear made them miss more. I've seen the same thing off the court — people who shrink themselves because they're afraid of failing again, people who avoid opportunities because the last one hurt, people who stop trusting themselves after one painful outcome.

But you can't play your best tennis — or live your best life — while trying not to lose. Second serves, just like second chances, require courage. Both ask you to swing with intention, not fear. Both ask you to trust that you're more than your last mistake.

And you are.

The Real Lesson

"The first serve is who you want to be. The second serve is who you really are."

Anyone can look confident when everything is going well. But who are you when the pressure hits? Who are you when you've already missed once? Who are you when the margin is thin, and the stakes feel high? That's where growth happens. That's where resilience is built. That's where character is revealed. And that's where your life begins to change.

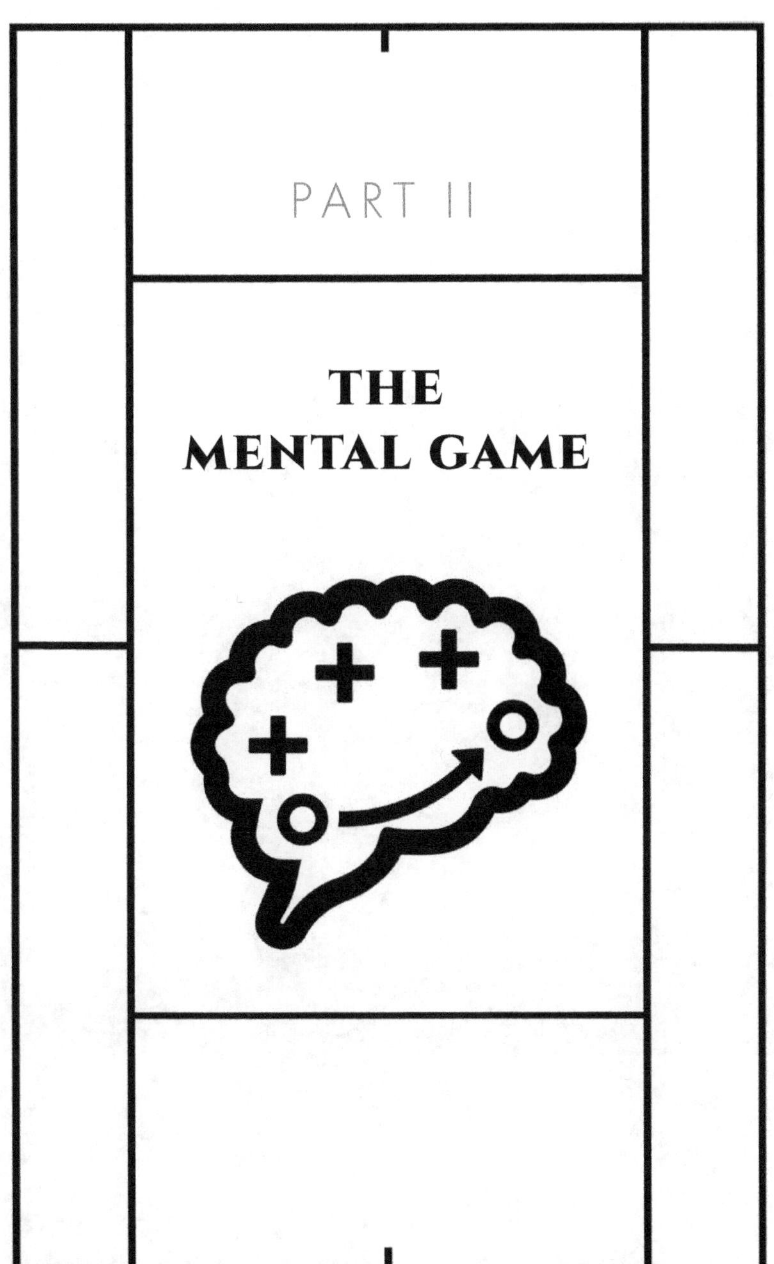

PART II

THE MENTAL GAME

CHAPTER 7

Rebuilding Confidence After Mistakes

***

How to Reset, Recover, and Rise Stronger

Confidence is a fragile thing. It takes weeks, months, sometimes years to build — and one bad moment to shake. Every player knows this feeling: You miss a serve you normally make, or you botch a shot you've hit a thousand times, and suddenly your mind starts whispering, "What if I can't do this anymore?"

And if you're human — which you are — you've felt the same thing in life.

Confidence doesn't disappear because you're weak. It disappears because you care. But here's the truth most people never learn: Confidence isn't something you lose — it's something you rebuild.

And rebuilding it is a skill.

1. The Confidence Dip: Why It Happens

Confidence drops for the same reasons double faults happen:

- Pressure
- Fear
- Overthinking
- Emotional residue from past mistakes

When you miss a serve, your brain doesn't just see the miss — it sees the memory of every miss you've ever made. That's how the mind works. It protects you by reminding you of danger, even when the danger is just a tennis ball.

In life, the same pattern shows up:

- One rejection triggers memories of every rejection
- One argument triggers memories of every conflict
- One failure triggers memories of every setback

Your brain isn't trying to sabotage you — it's trying to keep you safe. But safety and confidence rarely live in the same place.

2. The Reset: What Great Players Do Differently

The best players in the world don't avoid confidence dips — they recover from them faster.

Here's what they do: They reset immediately.

A deep breath. A small routine. A moment of stillness. They don't let the mistake bleed into the next point. They separate the mistake from their identity. Missing a serve doesn't mean you're a bad server. Failing once doesn't mean you're a failure. They return to fundamentals.

When confidence drops, simplicity saves you:

- Slow the toss
- Trust the motion
- Hit your targets

In life, fundamentals look like:

- Sleep
- Movement
- Honest conversations
- Grounding routines

Confidence grows from stability.

3. The Rebuild: How Confidence Actually Returns

Confidence doesn't come back all at once. It returns in layers.

Layer 1: Small Wins

A safe second serve. A clean rally ball. A simple decision executed well.

Small wins rebuild trust.

Layer 2: Consistency

Confidence grows when you show yourself you can repeat success — even tiny success.

Layer 3: Courage

Eventually, you have to take a risk again. A bigger serve. A bolder choice. A tougher conversation.

Courage is the bridge between who you were and who you're becoming.

4. The Stories We Tell Ourselves

Confidence is built or broken by the stories you repeat in your head.

The destructive story:

"I always mess this up."
"I'm not good enough."
"I can't handle pressure."

The empowering story:

"I've done this before."
"I know how to adjust."
"I can handle this moment."

The story you choose becomes the reality you live.

5. Confidence in Life: The Same Rules Apply

Confidence in life is rebuilt the same way it's rebuilt in tennis:

- Acknowledge the mistake
- Reset your mindset
- Return to fundamentals
- Build small wins
- Take courageous steps
- Rewrite the story

Confidence isn't a personality trait — it's a practice.

6. The Real Lesson

Confidence isn't about never doubting yourself. It's about knowing how to find yourself again after doubt shows up.

It's about:

- Resilience
- Awareness
- Patience
- Repetition
- Courage

And most importantly, it's about remembering this: You are always one good swing away from feeling like yourself again.

CHAPTER 8

Playing Under Pressure

***

How to Stay Centered When Everything Feels Heavy

Pressure is one of the most misunderstood forces in tennis — and in life. People talk about it like it's an enemy, something to avoid or fear. But pressure isn't the problem. Pressure is a sign that something matters. It's a sign that you're in the arena, not sitting safely on the sidelines.

The real challenge isn't pressure itself. It's how you respond to it.

Some players tighten up. Some players rush. Some players overthink. Some players collapse under the weight of their own expectations. And then there are the players who learn to breathe inside the moment. Those who learn to stay present, who learn to trust themselves when everything feels loud.

Those players don't avoid pressure — they use it.

1. What Pressure Really Is

Pressure is simply the gap between expectation and belief.

- Expectation: What you think you should do.
- Belief: What you think you're capable of doing.

When expectation rises faster than belief, pressure spikes. In tennis, this shows up as:

- Serving at 30–40
- Closing out a set

- Playing in front of a crowd
- Facing a rival you've never beaten

In life, it shows up as:

- Job interviews
- Big decisions
- Difficult conversations
- Moments where you feel judged

Pressure isn't a flaw — it's feedback. It tells you where your belief needs to grow.

2. The Body's Response to Pressure

When pressure hits, your body reacts before your mind does.

- Your heart rate jumps
- Your breathing shortens
- Your muscles tighten
- Your thoughts speed up

This is your nervous system trying to protect you. But protection and performance don't always align. A tight body can't swing freely. A racing mind can't make clear decisions. A panicked breath can't support a calm serve.

Learning to manage pressure starts with learning to manage your physiology.

3. The Power of Presence

The players who handle pressure best aren't fearless — they're present. They don't think about the last point. They don't think about the next point. They don't think about the crowd, the score, or the stakes. They think about the ball. The target. The breath. The moment.

Presence is a skill. And like any skill, it can be trained.

Tools for presence:

- Deep breathing: Slow exhale, long inhale
- Focal points: Pick a target and commit to it
- Routines: Let your habits carry you when your mind gets loud
- Mantras: Short, grounding phrases like “one point” or “trust it”

Presence shrinks pressure down to something you can handle.

4. The Stories We Tell Under Pressure

Pressure amplifies whatever story you already believe about yourself.

If your story is:

- “I always choke,”
- “I’m not good enough,”
- Or, “I can’t handle big moments,”

then pressure will expose that story.

But if your story is:

- “I adjust,”
- “I compete,”
- Or, “I stay in the moment,”

then pressure becomes fuel.

The story you choose becomes the performance you deliver.

5. Pressure in Life: The Same Patterns

Life has its own tiebreakers:

- The job you really want
- The conversation you've been avoiding
- The opportunity you're scared to take
- The moment where your future shifts

And just like in tennis, pressure doesn't mean you're unprepared — it means you're stepping into something meaningful.

Life under pressure requires:

- Grounding
- Clarity
- Breath
- Intention
- Trust

The same tools that help you serve at 5–6 in a tiebreak help you speak up in a meeting, ask for what you need, or take a risk that scares you.

6. The Real Lesson

Pressure isn't the villain. Pressure is the invitation.

It's the moment that asks:

- Will you trust yourself?
- Will you stay present?
- Will you breathe?
- Will you swing?
- Will you show up?

You don't become stronger by avoiding pressure. You become stronger by learning to stand inside it without losing yourself. And once you learn that skill — on the court or in life — everything changes.

CHAPTER 9

When the Match Slips Away

***

How to Stay Mentally Tough When Everything Feels Like It's Going Wrong

Every player knows the feeling: You start a match strong, you're moving well, you're seeing the ball cleanly — and then suddenly, something shifts. A few errors creep in. Your opponent heats up. Your timing feels off. The scoreboard turns against you. And before you know it, you're not just playing your opponent anymore — you're fighting yourself.

Life has moments like this, too. Moments where things unravel faster than you can process. Moments where you feel like you're losing ground, no matter what you do. The real test isn't whether you can dominate when things are going well. The real test is whether you can stay composed when the match starts slipping away.

This chapter is about that test.

Matches don't fall apart all at once. They slip away slowly — a point here, a rushed decision there, a moment where your mind starts running faster than your feet. Before you know it, you're no longer playing the match in front of you. You're playing the one in your head.

The spiral always starts quietly. Maybe you rush between points. Maybe you get a little too quiet, or a little too emotional. Maybe you start swinging faster than your mind can keep up. Maybe you drift away from the patterns that usually anchor you. It doesn't look dramatic at first — it just feels like you're slightly out of sync.

Life has its own version of this. You snap at someone you care about. You make a quick decision you regret. You shut down instead of speaking up. You overthink until you're exhausted. You drift away from the routines that keep you steady. The first step to stopping the spiral — in tennis or in life — is simply noticing that it's happening.

When a match starts slipping, most players do the exact opposite of what they need. They speed up. They try to fix everything at once. They want to erase the mistake, outrun the discomfort, and get back to safety as fast as possible. But speeding up is the worst thing you can do. The moment you rush, you lose the ability to think clearly.

The pause is your lifeline. A deep breath. A slow walk back to the baseline. A moment to let your shoulders drop. A second to reconnect with your intention. The pause isn't weakness — it's control. It's the moment where you reclaim the match instead of letting the match claim you.

Life works the same way. Sometimes the smartest thing you can do is step away from the argument, take a walk before responding, breathe before reacting, or give yourself a little space to think. The pause is where clarity returns.

When things go wrong, players often abandon the very things that make them good. They start hitting shots they don't own. They force winners. They try to play like someone else. They react emotionally instead of strategically. It's an instinct — when you're panicking, you reach for anything that feels like a shortcut out of the moment.

The real key to stopping the slide is returning to your identity by figuring out:

- What patterns do you trust?
- What shots feel like home?
- What tempo allows you to breathe?
- What mindset helps you compete?

In life, identity matters just as much:

- Who are you when you're grounded?
- What values guide you?
- What habits keep you stable?
- What version of yourself do you want to show up as?

When you return to your identity, you return to your power. When a match starts slipping away, the moment feels enormous. The stakes feel heavier. The pressure feels suffocating. But the truth is simple: You can only play one point at a time. The moment shrinks when your focus shrinks. One serve. One target. One breath. One decision. That's all you ever control.

Life is no different. When everything feels overwhelming, zoom in. One task. One conversation. One step. One choice. You don't win the match by staring at the finish line. You win it by winning the next point.

And then there are the emotions — the frustration, the fear, the anger, the embarrassment, the doubt. These emotions are normal, but they're rarely helpful. Champions aren't emotionless; they're emotionally neutral. Neutrality sounds like, "Okay, that happened. Next point. I can adjust. Stay here." Neutrality keeps you in the match. Emotion pulls you out of it. In life, neutrality is the difference between reacting and responding.

Comebacks don't happen because players suddenly become better. They happen because players stop making things worse. They stop feeding the spiral. They slow down. They breathe. They simplify. They return to what they trust. They give themselves a chance to rebuild.

Life's comebacks work the same way. You stabilize. You breathe. You simplify. You rebuild. You start trusting yourself again. Comebacks aren't built on miracles — they're built on small, steady choices made in the right direction.

And the moment you stop spiraling, you start returning.

CHAPTER 10

Identity on the Court

***

Who You Become When the Pressure Hits

Every player has a version of themselves they want to be on the court — confident, composed, aggressive, fearless. But the version that actually shows up under pressure? That's the real you. Not the polished version. Not the idealized version. The honest version. And that version is worth studying.

Because the truth is simple: Tennis doesn't just test your skills — it reveals your identity.

And life does the same.

1. **The Player You Think You Are vs. The Player You Become**

   Most players have a mental image of themselves:

   - "I'm an aggressive baseliner."
   - "I'm mentally tough."
   - "I'm consistent."
   - "I'm a fighter."

   But when the match gets tight, that identity gets tested. Under pressure, you learn:

   - Whether you trust your patterns
   - Whether you stay patient
   - Whether you panic
   - Whether you compete

- Whether you stay present
- Whether you fight or fold

Pressure strips away the stories and shows the truth. This isn't a bad thing — it's a gift. It gives you a mirror that most people never get.

2. Identity Isn't Built in Comfort — It's Built in Challenge

You don't discover who you are when you're winning 6–1, 6–1.

You discover who you are when:

- You're down a break
- You've double-faulted twice
- Your legs feel heavy
- Your mind is loud
- Your opponent won't go away

That's where identity forms.

Life works the same way. You don't learn who you are when everything is smooth. You learn who you are when things get messy.

3. The Three Identities Every Player Has

1. The Practice Identity

This is the version of you that hits clean, relaxed, confident balls when no one is watching.

It's your potential.

2. The Match Identity

This is the version of you that shows up when the scoreboard matters.

It's your reality.

3. The Pressure Identity

This is the version of you that appears when everything is on the line. It's your truth.

The goal isn't to eliminate the gap between these identities — it's to understand them. Because once you understand them, you can train them.

4. Training Your Identity

Identity isn't fixed. It's shaped by repetition, awareness, and intention.

To train your identity, you must:

A. *Know your patterns*

- Do you rush?
- Do you tighten?
- Do you get passive?
- Do you get reckless?

Awareness is the first step.

B. *Build habits that hold under pressure*

Your identity is built from what you repeat:

- Routines
- Breathing
- Targets
- Patterns
- Self-talk

These become your anchors.

C. *Practice the version of yourself you want to become*

- If you want to be calm under pressure, practice calmness.
- If you want to be aggressive, practice aggression.

- If you want to be resilient, practice resilience.
- Identity is trained the same way footwork is trained — through reps.

The Identity You Bring Into Life

The same identities show up outside the court.

Your "practice identity" in life: Who you are when things are easy.

Your "match identity" in life: Who you are when responsibilities show up.

Your "pressure identity" in life: Who you are when everything feels heavy.

The goal isn't perfection — it's alignment. You want the version of yourself you admire to be the version that shows up when it matters.

The Real Lesson

"Identity isn't something you discover once — it's something you build every day."

Every match, every mistake, every comeback, every moment of pressure is shaping you. Not into someone perfect, but into someone aware. Someone grounded, someone who knows who they are when the stakes rise. Because the truth is this: "You don't rise to the level of your goals — you fall to the level of your identity."

When you build an identity you trust, you stop fearing pressure. You stop fearing mistakes. You stop fearing the moment. You start playing — and living — with freedom.

You've just explored identity — who you become under pressure, who you are when the match tightens, and how your patterns shape your performance. But identity alone isn't enough. Knowing who you are is one thing. Staying grounded in that identity over time — through long matches, long struggles, long seasons — that's something else entirely.

Tennis isn't just a game of moments, it's a game of endurance, and life is no different.

So now we shift from identity to stamina — not physical stamina, but emotional stamina. The kind that keeps you steady when the match stretches on, and the outcome is still unclear.

Let's talk about the long game.

CHAPTER 11

EMOTIONAL ENDURANCE

***

HOW TO STAY STEADY IN THE LONG GAME OF TENNIS — AND LIFE

Anyone can be strong for a moment. Anyone can be confident for a point. Anyone can be composed for a few minutes. But the players who truly separate themselves — the ones who win the long matches, the long rallies, the long seasons — are the ones who know how to stay emotionally steady over time. That's emotional endurance. And it's one of the most underrated skills in both tennis and life.

Long matches have a way of revealing everything about you. They show your patience, your discipline, your emotional habits, your ability to reset, and your ability to stay present when the match refuses to end. In a long match, you can't rely on adrenaline or momentum or that fleeting feeling of "playing well." You have to rely on something deeper — your ability to stay centered when the hours and the mind starts to wander.

Emotional endurance is what keeps you steady when the match drags on. It's what helps you stay focused when your thoughts drift, stay composed when frustration builds, stay committed when your legs get heavy, and stay intentional when you're tempted to rush. It's not glamorous, but it's powerful. It's the quiet strength that keeps you in the fight long after the excitement fades.

Every long match comes with emotional waves. One moment you feel confident, the next you're doubting everything.

One moment you're energized, the next you're exhausted. One moment you're clear, the next you're confused. Patience turns into frustration. Belief turns into fear.

Most players get tossed around by those waves. Great players learn to surf them. They don't panic when doubt shows up. They don't collapse when frustration hits. They don't assume the match is slipping away just because they feel off for a few games. They understand something essential: Emotions are temporary, but decisions are permanent.

That's where neutrality comes in. Neutrality is the anchor of emotional endurance. It doesn't mean you're numb or passive or emotionless. It means you don't overreact. You don't catastrophize. You don't spiral. You don't let one moment bleed into the next. Neutrality is the ability to say, "Okay. That happened. Now what?" It's the mindset that keeps you in the match when everything inside you wants to run.

The middle of a match is where most players lose themselves. Not the beginning, when everything feels fresh. Not the end, when adrenaline kicks back in. The middle — that long, messy stretch where fatigue sets in, doubt creeps in, the score tightens, the mind gets loud, and the body feels heavier than it should. The middle is where emotional endurance matters most.

Managing the middle is about simplifying. It's about slowing your breathing, narrowing your focus, trusting the patterns you've built, and giving yourself permission to be patient. It's about staying present when your mind wants to jump ahead or drift away. The middle is where champions are built — not because they play perfect tennis, but because they refuse to abandon themselves.

Life has long matches, too. Long seasons of uncertainty. Long stretches of stress. Long periods of growth that feel more like struggle. Long waits for clarity. Long battles with self-doubt. And just like in tennis, emotional endurance is what carries you through. Life asks you to be patient when things don't move fast. It asks you to stay disciplined when motivation fades. It asks you to find clarity when emotions cloud your vision. It asks you to be resilient when setbacks pile up. It asks you to stay present when the future feels overwhelming.

Emotional endurance is the ability to stay grounded when life stretches you. It's the strength to keep showing up — not with perfection, but with presence. Emotional endurance isn't about being strong all the time. It's about staying steady enough to keep going.

So the truth is this: You don't win long matches by being perfect — you win them by staying in them. And the same is true for life.

You've just explored emotional endurance — the ability to stay steady through long matches, long struggles, and long seasons. But endurance alone isn't enough. You can be steady, patient, and disciplined, yet still feel lost if you don't know why you're fighting.

Every player reaches a point where effort isn't the issue — clarity is.

When the match stretches on...
When the setbacks pile up...
When the progress feels slow...
When the pressure gets heavy...

You need something deeper than technique or toughness. You need purpose. So now we shift from endurance to meaning — from how you stay steady to why you keep going. Let's talk about the deeper "why" behind your game, your growth, and your life.

CHAPTER 12

PLAYING WITH PURPOSE

***

WHY YOUR "WHY" MATTERS MORE THAN YOUR WINS

Every player has a reason they step on the court. Some play for competition. Some play for fun. Some play for identity. Some play for escape. Some play because tennis gives them something that nothing else does. And the same is true in life.

Purpose isn't a slogan. Purpose is fuel. Purpose is direction. Purpose is the anchor that keeps you grounded when everything else feels shaky. When you know your "why," you don't crumble as easily. You don't panic as quickly. You don't quit as often. Purpose gives your effort meaning.

A player without a personal "why" is like a serve without a target — powerful, maybe, but directionless. Purpose is what gives your effort shape. It's what gives your work meaning. It's what gives your fight a reason to exist. When you know why you're out there, the match stops feeling like something you're surviving and starts feeling like something you're choosing.

Purpose gives you clarity when your mind gets noisy. It gives you resilience when the match stretches longer than you expected. It gives you motivation when your energy dips. It gives you emotional stability when the pressure spikes. It gives you a reason to keep going when everything in you wants to walk away.

Your “why” doesn’t have to be dramatic. It doesn’t have to impress anyone. It just has to be honest. Maybe you play to grow. Maybe you play to compete. Maybe you play to express yourself, or to challenge yourself, or to feel alive. Maybe you’re trying to prove something to yourself. Maybe you’re trying to build confidence. Maybe you’re searching for peace. Maybe you’re trying to connect with something — or someone — through the game. Whatever your reason is, it’s valid. It’s yours.

And when pressure hits, that purpose becomes your anchor. Players who chase only results crumble when the scoreboard turns against them. But players who play for something deeper stay grounded. They remind themselves, “I’m here to compete. I’m here to grow. I’m here to challenge myself. I’m here to stay present.”

Purpose shifts your focus from outcome to intention — and intention is what keeps you steady when the match gets loud.

Every player reaches moments where they want to walk off the court — physically or emotionally. Moments where the match feels too long, the mistakes feel too heavy, the pressure feels too loud, the doubt feels too real. Purpose doesn’t remove those moments. It simply reminds you why they’re worth facing. It gives you a reason to stay in the match even when the match stops feeling kind.

Life has its own matches — careers, relationships, personal growth, setbacks, transitions, reinventions. And just like in tennis, purpose is what keeps you grounded through all of it. Purpose gives you direction when you feel lost, strength when you feel tired, clarity when you feel overwhelmed, and resilience when discouragement starts to pile up.

Purpose doesn't make life easier. It makes life meaningful. And here's something most people don't realize: Purpose isn't something you find once and keep forever. It shifts. It evolves. It grows with you.

Sometimes players lose their purpose. Sometimes people do too. That's not failure — that's being human. When you feel disconnected from your purpose, you don't need to force an answer. You just need to start asking the right questions. What matters to you now? What energizes you? What challenges you in a way that feels good? What do you want to build? Who are you becoming?

Purpose isn't a destination. It's a relationship — one you return to again and again as you change, as you grow, as you learn more about who you are and what you want. Purpose gives you meaning, and meaning is what makes the journey worth taking.

You've just explored purpose — the deeper "why" behind your effort, your growth, and your resilience. Purpose gives you direction. Purpose gives you meaning. Purpose gives you something to hold onto when the match gets tough.

The truth is, purpose alone isn't enough.

You can know why you're fighting ...

You can know what you want ...

You can know who you want to become ...

... but if you don't trust yourself to execute, none of it sticks.

Self-trust is the bridge between intention and action. Between belief and performance. Between who you are and who you're becoming. So now we shift from purpose to trust — the quiet, powerful force that holds your entire mental game together.

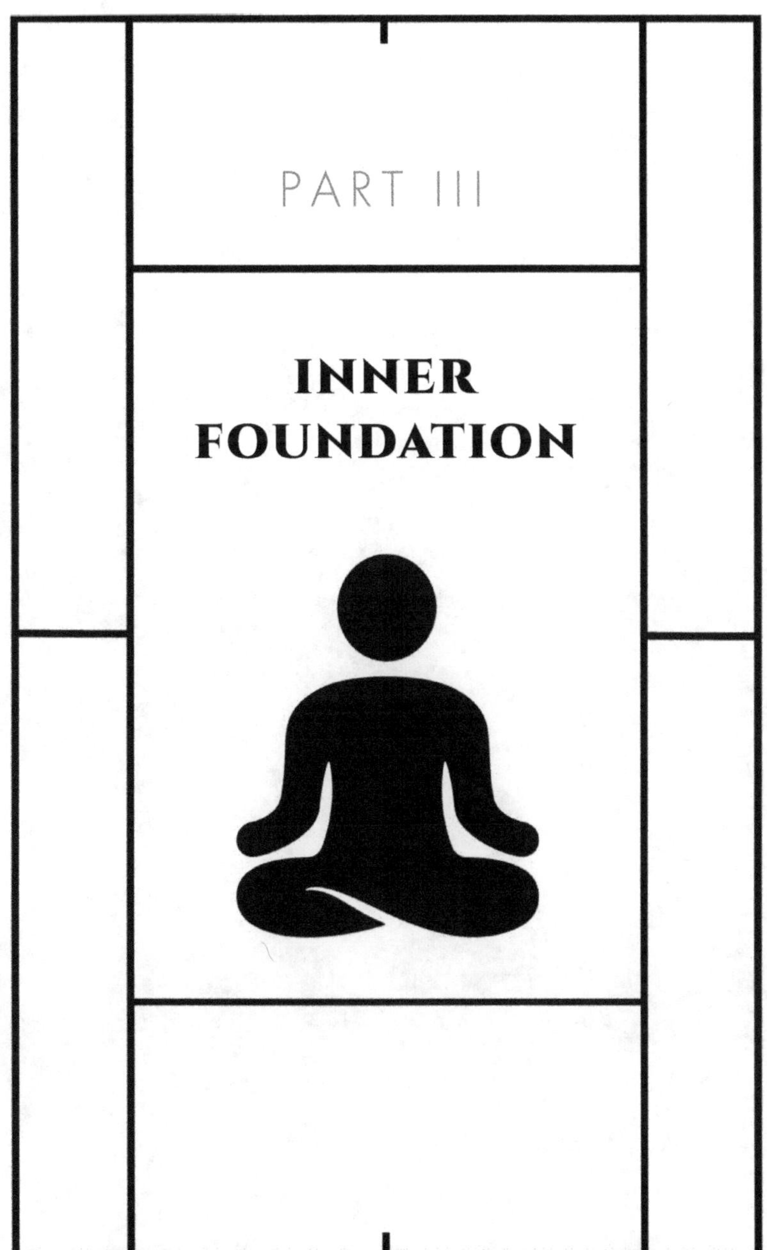
PART III
INNER FOUNDATION

CHAPTER 13

SELF-TRUST

***

THE FOUNDATION OF EVERY CONFIDENT SWING

If there's one thing I've seen over and over — in juniors, adults, college players, even pros — it's this: The players who perform best under pressure aren't the ones with the prettiest strokes or the biggest weapons. They're the ones who trust themselves. Self-trust is the foundation of confidence. It's the backbone of resilience. It's the anchor of mental toughness. Without self-trust, everything becomes shaky. With self-trust, everything becomes possible.

Self-trust is one of the most misunderstood skills in the mental game. People confuse it with arrogance, or with pretending you're perfect, or with some kind of blind confidence that never wavers. But real self-trust is quieter than that. It's steadier. It's the belief that you can handle the moment you're in. That you can adjust when things shift. That you can recover when you slip. That you can rely on the patterns you've built. That you can stay composed even when the pressure rises.

Self-trust is knowing that even if things go wrong, you won't abandon yourself. And here's the truth: You're not born with that kind of trust. No one is. You build it. You build it through repetition — through showing up again and again until the unfamiliar becomes familiar. Every rep is a small vote for the player you want to become. You build it through honesty — by being real about your strengths and your weaknesses instead of pretending they don't exist. You build it through consistency — through habits that show your mind, "I can rely on myself." And you build it through recovery — every time you bounce back from a mistake, you reinforce the belief, I can handle this.

"Self-trust grows through small wins, not grand gestures."

But just like it can be built, it can be broken. Self-trust cracks when you overthink, when you panic, when you abandon your patterns, when you try to be someone you're not, when you judge yourself harshly, when you chase perfection. But the biggest killer of self-trust is trying to control outcomes instead of controlling your actions. The moment you tie your identity to results, you stop trusting your process. You stop trusting yourself.

When self-trust is strong, it creates a powerful loop. Trust leads to freedom. Freedom leads to better execution. Better execution creates evidence. And evidence builds more trust. That loop is the engine of confidence. It's why some players look so fluid under pressure — they're not guessing who they are. They're not negotiating with themselves. They trust their swing, so they swing freely.

Pressure exposes your relationship with yourself more than anything else. Players who don't trust themselves guide the ball, play scared, overthink, tighten up, avoid risk, and panic after mistakes. Players who do trust themselves commit to their patterns, swing with intention, stay present, adjust without fear, recover quickly, and stay emotionally neutral. Self-trust is the difference between surviving pressure and thriving in it.

Life tests your self-trust the same way tennis does. Speaking up requires self-trust. Taking risks requires self-trust. Ending something that isn't right requires self-trust. Starting something new requires self-trust. Making decisions without certainty requires self-trust. Choosing growth over comfort requires self-trust. It's the belief that you can navigate the unknown — not because you know the outcome, but because you know yourself.

If you've lost trust in yourself, that's not a failure. It's a sign that you've lived. It's a sign that you've tried. And the good news is that self-trust can always be rebuilt. You rebuild it by keeping small promises to yourself. By returning to your routines. By simplifying your decisions. By forgiving your mistakes. By noticing your progress. By practicing presence. By practicing patience. Self-trust grows quietly, steadily, and honestly.

At the end of the day, self-trust is the foundation of everything — confidence, resilience, composure, identity, purpose, performance. It's the belief that no matter what happens — win or lose, succeed or fail — you will not abandon yourself. You don't need to be perfect to trust yourself. You just need to be present, honest, and willing to keep showing up.

You've just explored self-trust — the foundation of confidence, resilience, and composure. But even with strong self-trust, there will be moments when things don't go your way. Moments where the match turns. Moments where your body feels off. Moments where your mind gets loud. Moments where life throws something at you that you didn't choose.

And this is where many players — and many people — get stuck.

They fight reality. They resist the moment. They tighten up. They panic. They try to force control where control doesn't exist.

But the truth is simple: You can't play your best tennis — or live your best life — while fighting the moment you're in.

So now we shift from trust to acceptance — the skill that allows you to stay grounded even when things aren't going your way.

CHAPTER 14

ACCEPTANCE

***

THE STRENGTH OF LETTING THE MOMENT BE WHAT IT IS

Acceptance is a skill that is widely misunderstood in the mental game. People hear the word and think it means giving up, lowering their standards, or settling for less. But acceptance isn't surrender. Acceptance is clarity. It's the ability to look at the moment and say, "This is where I am. This is what's happening. This is the reality I'm working with." You don't have to like it. You just have to be willing to see it. Because you can't adjust to a reality you refuse to acknowledge.

When players resist reality, they spiral. They start telling themselves stories — "I shouldn't be missing this. I can't believe this is happening. This match should be easier. Why am I playing so badly?" That resistance creates tension. The tension creates mistakes. The mistakes create frustration. The frustration creates more resistance. And suddenly the match feels heavier than it needs to be.

Life works the same way. When you resist setbacks, emotions, uncertainty, change, or discomfort, you make the moment harder than it already is. You add weight to something that was already challenging. You fight the moment instead of working with it. Acceptance creates space — emotional space, mental space, breathing room. When you accept the moment, you stop fighting it. When you stop fighting it, you stop wasting energy. And when you stop wasting energy, you start seeing clearly again. Acceptance is the reset button. It's the moment where your shoulders drop, your breath deepens, and your mind comes back online.

Acceptance isn't the end of the process — it's the beginning. Once you accept the moment, you can finally ask the right questions. What's the smartest play right now? What can I actually control? What needs to change? What can I let go of? Acceptance opens the door to adjustment. Adjustment leads to improvement. Improvement creates momentum. And momentum is how comebacks begin.

Life demands acceptance just as much as tennis does. Acceptance in life looks like acknowledging your emotions without judging them, recognizing when something isn't working, letting go of unrealistic expectations, accepting that growth is messy, accepting that progress isn't linear, and accepting that you're human. Acceptance doesn't weaken you — it frees you. It frees you from perfection. It frees you from pressure. It frees you from the stories that keep you stuck.

Acceptance is also an act of self-compassion. It's the moment you say, "I'm allowed to struggle. I'm allowed to be imperfect. I'm allowed to adjust. I'm allowed to grow." Self-compassion isn't softness. It's strength — the strength to stay in the match even when you're not playing your best.

Acceptance isn't giving up. Acceptance is letting go of the fight with reality so you can fight for the point in front of you. It's the moment where tension releases, clarity returns, presence deepens, and adjustment becomes possible. Acceptance is the foundation of resilience. It's the skill that keeps you grounded when the match — or life — gets messy.

Because the truth is simple: You can't change a moment you refuse to accept; however, once you accept it, you can change everything that comes next.

You've just explored acceptance — the ability to face reality without collapsing, resisting, or spiraling. Acceptance gives you clarity. Acceptance gives you presence. Acceptance gives you the emotional space to adjust. Acceptance is only the beginning.

Once you accept the moment, the next step is learning how to let go — letting go of tension, letting go of fear, letting go of perfection, letting go of the stories that keep you tight and hesitant.

The truth is this: Most players don't lose because they lack skill. They lose because they hold on too tightly. So now we shift from acceptance to release — the skill that unlocks freedom, flow, and authentic performance.

CHAPTER 15

LETTING GO

***

RELEASING TENSION, FEAR, AND THE STORIES THAT HOLD YOU BACK

Letting go is one of the hardest skills in tennis — and in life. Not because it's complicated, but because it requires trust. Trust in your body. Trust in your preparation. Trust in the moment. Trust in yourself. Most players grip too tightly — physically, mentally, emotionally. They try to control everything. They try to force outcomes. They try to muscle their way through pressure. But the tighter you hold, the smaller you play. Letting go is the opposite of giving up. Letting go is permitting yourself to play freely.

Every player carries weight they never talk about. Fear of missing. Fear of losing. Fear of being judged. Fear of disappointing people. Fear of not being enough. None of it shows up on the scoreboard, but it shows up everywhere else. It shows up in tight shoulders, stiff swings, rushed footwork, and shallow breathing. It shows up in the mind too — in the overthinking, the catastrophizing, the self-criticism, the perfectionism. Letting go is the process of putting that weight down so you can actually play.

One of the biggest traps in tennis is the illusion of control. Players try to control everything — the outcome, the opponent, the conditions, the crowd, the bounce, the future. But the truth is simple: You can't control any of that. The only things you ever truly control are your intention, your effort, your patterns, your breath, your attitude, and your presence. Letting go means releasing everything that isn't yours to carry so you can focus on what is.

Letting go starts in the body. You can feel it when you're holding too tightly — the grip that turns into a vise, the swing that feels forced, the shoulders that creep up, the breath that gets shallow, the movement that stiffens. The body tells the truth long before the mind does. And the body also knows how to release. Shake out your arms. Loosen your grip. Exhale fully. Drop your shoulders. Slow your tempo. Soften your eyes. A relaxed body creates a free swing.

Now, physical letting go is only the beginning. Mental letting go is the ability to release the thoughts that don't serve you — the ones that tighten your mind the same way tension tightens your muscles. "I can't miss this. I always mess up here. I should be playing better. I can't lose to this person. Everyone is judging me."

These thoughts don't protect you. They trap you. Letting go means grounding yourself in simple cues, visualizing what you want to do, focusing on your targets, simplifying your decisions, and returning to your routines. A quiet mind creates clear decisions.

And then there's emotional letting go — the hardest and most important part. Frustration, embarrassment, anger, regret, fear ... these emotions can take over a match if you let them. But you don't release emotions by suppressing them. You release them by acknowledging them without letting them run the show. Acceptance, breath-work, self-compassion, reframing, presence — these are the tools that steady your heart. And a steady heart creates resilience.

Life demands letting go just as much as tennis does. Letting go of perfection. Letting go of timelines. Letting go of old identities. Letting go of past mistakes. Letting go of unrealistic expectations. Letting go of the need for approval. Letting go of the fear of being seen. Letting go of the fear of failing. Letting go doesn't make you weaker — it makes you lighter. It frees you to move forward. It frees you to grow. It frees you to become who you're meant to be.

Letting go isn't a single moment — it's a practice. It's the practice of releasing tension, fear, judgment, pressure, perfection, and control so you can return to freedom, flow, presence, trust, authenticity, and joy. Because the truth is this: You play your best tennis — and live your best life — when you stop gripping so tightly and start letting yourself breathe.

Letting go is the doorway to freedom. Freedom is the doorway to performance. Performance is the doorway to growth.

You've just explored letting go — releasing tension, fear, perfectionism, and the stories that keep you tight. Letting go frees your body. It frees your mind. It frees your emotions. But once you've let go, you need somewhere to land. And that place is the present moment.

The reality is this: You can't play freely if you're living in the past. You can't play confidently if you're living in the future. You can only play — and live — in the now.

So now we shift from letting go to presence — the skill that anchors everything you've learned so far.

CHAPTER 16

PRESENCE

***

THE ART OF COMPETING IN THE ONLY MOMENT THAT EXISTS

Presence is the heartbeat of great tennis. It's the quiet, powerful ability to stay fully engaged with the point in front of you — not the point you just lost, not the point you're afraid of losing next. Presence is the antidote to overthinking. Presence is the antidote to pressure. Presence is the antidote to fear. Presence is where your best tennis lives.

Presence is one of the most powerful skills in tennis, but it's also one of the most misunderstood. Presence isn't zoning out. It isn't pretending you don't care. It isn't ignoring your emotions or acting like the stakes don't matter. Presence is the ability to feel the moment without being swallowed by it. It's the ability to focus on what you can control, stay grounded in your body, stay connected to your intention, and respond instead of react. Presence is clarity. Presence is calm. Presence is power, but presence has enemies — and they're relentless.

The past tries to pull you backward. It shows up as regret, frustration, replay loops, and that familiar voice asking, "What was that shot? How did I miss that?" The future tries to pull you forward. It shows up as fear, anxiety, outcome thinking, and the spiral of "What if I lose? What if I choke? What if this goes wrong?" And then there's the ego — the sideways pull. Judgment. Comparison. Identity panic. "I shouldn't be struggling. I can't lose to this person."

"Presence is what pulls you back to center."

Presence always begins in the body. Not the mind. When you're present, your body feels grounded, balanced, rhythmic, connected, responsive. When you're not present, your body tells the truth — it tightens, rushes, jerks, disconnects, feels heavy. The body is the doorway to the moment. A deep exhale. Softer eyes. A relaxed grip. A steadier tempo. A grounded stance. These small physical cues bring you back faster than any thought ever could.

Presence in the mind is simpler than people think. It's the ability to focus on one thing at a time. One target. One pattern. One breath. One mantra. One routine. Presence is simplicity. It's narrowing your attention to what matters and letting everything else fall away.

Presence in emotion is where the real work happens. Presence doesn't mean you stop feeling. It means you stop drowning in what you feel. You name the emotion. You breathe through it. You let it move without resisting. You return to your intention. Emotion becomes manageable the moment you stop fighting it.

And then there's presence under pressure — the real test. Pressure tries to drag you out of the moment. Presence pulls you back in. Players who stay present under pressure breathe more slowly, move more smoothly, think more clearly, swing more freely, and adjust more quickly. Presence is the difference between reacting and responding. It's the difference between tightening and trusting.

Life demands presence just as much as tennis does. Presence in life looks like listening fully, speaking intentionally, slowing down, noticing your emotions, choosing your actions, and being where your feet are. Presence makes relationships deeper. It makes decisions clearer. It makes life richer.

Presence is the foundation of freedom. Freedom is the foundation of performance. Performance is the foundation of growth. Presence is the moment where the noise quiets, the fear softens, the tension releases, the mind clears, and the body flows. The truth is this: Your best tennis — and your best life — only exist in the present moment. Everything else is a distraction. Presence is where you meet your potential. Presence is where you meet yourself.

You've just explored presence — the ability to stay grounded in the only moment that exists. Presence is the foundation of clarity, calm, and intentional action. But presence is also the doorway to something even more powerful.

When you combine presence with trust ...

When you combine trust with acceptance ...

When you combine acceptance with letting go ...

When you combine letting go with emotional steadiness ...

You enter a different state entirely.

A state where the game feels lighter. A state where decisions feel natural. A state where your body moves before your mind even speaks. A state where you're not forcing anything — you're simply flowing. This is the state every athlete chases. This is the state every human recognizes when they feel fully alive. So now we shift from presence to flow — the pinnacle of mental performance.

CHAPTER 17

Flow

***

The State Where Tennis — and Life — Become Effortless

Flow is the holy grail of performance. It's the moment where everything feels connected. Where your body moves without hesitation. Where your mind is quiet. Where time slows down. Where the game feels like it's playing through you, not just by you. Flow isn't magic — it's alignment. It's the natural result of all the mental skills you've built so far.

- Presence.
- Letting go.
- Acceptance.
- Self-trust.
- Identity.
- Purpose.
- Emotional endurance.

"Flow is what happens when all of these pieces click into place."

1. What Flow Really Is

Flow is a state of deep engagement. It's not hype. It's not adrenaline. It's not "trying harder."

Flow is:

- Calm intensity
- Effortless focus

- Smooth movement
- Instinctive decision-making
- Emotional neutrality
- Full immersion in the moment

Flow is the absence of friction.

2. How Flow Feels in Tennis

When you're in flow:

- The ball looks bigger
- The court feels slower
- Your swing feels natural
- Your footwork feels automatic
- Your decisions feel obvious
- Your mind feels quiet

You're not thinking — you're responding. You're not forcing — you're allowing. You're not trying to win — you're simply playing.

Flow is the purest form of tennis.

3. The Conditions That Create Flow

Flow doesn't happen by accident. It happens when certain conditions align.

A. *Presence*

You're fully in the moment.

B. Challenge-Skill Balance

The task is hard enough to engage you, but not so hard that it overwhelms you.

C. Clear Intention

You know what you're trying to do.

D. Emotional Neutrality

You're not judging yourself.

E. Letting Go

You're not gripping too tightly.

F. Trust

You're allowing your training to take over. Flow is the natural outcome of mental alignment.

4. What Breaks Flow

Flow is fragile. It can break quickly if you're not aware.

Flow breaks when:

- You start thinking about the score
- You start judging your performance
- You start forcing shots
- You start fearing mistakes
- You start living in the past or future

Flow requires presence. Presence requires trust. Trust requires letting go.

5. How to Return to Flow

You can't force flow — but you can invite it.

Tools to return to flow:

- Slow your breath
- Simplify your targets
- Return to your patterns
- Soften your grip

- Ground your feet
- Use your routines
- Release judgment
- Reconnect with your intention

Flow returns when you stop chasing it.

6. Flow in Life

Flow isn't just a tennis state — it's a life state.

You feel flow when:

- You're writing
- You're creating
- You're teaching
- You're problem-solving
- You're connecting deeply with someone
- You're fully immersed in what you're doing

Flow is the feeling of being alive, aligned, and engaged. It's the moment where your skills, your purpose, and your presence merge.

7. The Real Lesson

Flow isn't something you achieve — it's something you allow.

It's the natural expression of:

- Trust
- Presence
- Acceptance
- Letting go
- Identity
- Purpose
- Emotional steadiness

Flow is the reward for doing the inner work. Flow is the state where your potential becomes real. Flow is the moment where tennis — and life — feel effortless.

The truth is simple: You don't enter flow by trying harder. You enter flow by getting out of your own way.

Flow is the peak of performance — the state where everything feels effortless, aligned, and alive. But flow isn't permanent. It comes and goes. It rises and fades. It's a gift, not a guarantee. And this is where many players get confused. They think flow should last forever. They think losing flow means something is wrong. They think the goal is to stay in that perfect state all the time.

But the truth is this: Flow is a moment. Resilience is a lifestyle.

Flow helps you play your best. Resilience helps you survive the moments when you're nowhere near your best.

So now we shift from flow to resilience — the skill that keeps you grounded, steady, and moving forward no matter what the match or life throws at you.

PART IV

THE PLAYER YOU BECOME

CHAPTER 18

Resilience

***

The Ability to Rise, Reset, and Respond

Resilience isn't about being tough all the time. It's not about pretending you're fine. It's not about pushing through everything with brute force. There's a moment in every match — sometimes early, sometimes late — where things stop going your way. The ball feels heavier. The court feels bigger. Your timing slips. Your confidence flickers. And suddenly you're standing there with a choice you didn't ask for.

Do you tighten ... or do you stay with yourself?

That moment is where resilience begins ...

Most people think resilience is loud — a fist pump, a roar, a heroic turnaround. But the real thing is almost invisible. It's quieter than people expect. It's the breath you take after a double fault. It's the decision to walk to the line instead of walking away from yourself. It's the small, steady "I'm still here" that you whisper internally when everything feels shaky.

Resilience isn't about avoiding difficulty. It's about meeting difficulty without losing your center. It's the art of navigating the mess without letting the mess define you. Sometimes that means adjusting your patterns. Sometimes it means slowing down. Sometimes it means trusting yourself even when doubt is loud. Sometimes it simply means staying present for one more point.

I've seen players who look unbreakable fall apart the moment things get uncomfortable. And I've seen players who look fragile become absolute steel when the match turns against them. The difference isn't talent, technique or confidence, it's recovery. Not the dramatic kind — the subtle kind. The kind where you let go of the last point before it poisons the next one. The kind where you release frustration before it becomes tension. The kind where you reset your breath before your mind starts sprinting ahead of you. Recovery is resilience in motion.

Adaptability is another form of resilience — the willingness to shift without losing yourself. The match changes. The conditions change. Your opponent changes. Your body changes. And resilience is the ability to adjust your plan without abandoning your identity. It's intelligence expressed through flexibility.

And then there's *persistence* — the most underestimated form of resilience. Persistence isn't stubbornness. It's not grinding for the sake of grinding. It's the quiet decision to keep showing up, point after point, even when the match feels long and your belief feels thin.

Persistence is the heartbeat of resilience. But resilience reveals itself most clearly in the tough moments — the ones you don't script. Down a break. Momentum gone. Opponent red-hot. Body heavy. Mind loud. Confidence shaky. These moments don't expose your weaknesses; they expose your relationship with yourself. They show whether you stay, whether you breathe, whether you trust, whether you continue.

Emotional resilience is its own world. It's not about suppressing what you feel. It's about letting emotions move through you without letting them take over. Frustration can visit without becoming your identity. Fear can show up without freezing you. Doubt can whisper without collapsing you. Pressure can rise without drowning you. Emotional resilience is honesty paired with steadiness.

In life — life demands resilience in ways tennis never could. Life stretches you. It tests your patience. It rearranges your plans. It hands you uncertainty without warning. It asks you to rebuild when you're tired and to trust yourself when the path isn't clear. Life resilience is the ability to keep moving through long seasons of growth, even when the growth doesn't feel good.

Resilience isn't built in dramatic moments. It's built in the small, unglamorous repetitions — the daily practice of presence, acceptance, letting go, self-trust, neutrality, recovery, patience. It's built in the way you talk to yourself after a mistake. It's built in the way you return to your routines. It's built in the way you choose to stay with yourself when it would be easier to check out.

Resilience isn't about being unbreakable. It's about being rebuildable. It's the ability to reset. To adjust. To breathe. To trust. To stay. To continue. Not because it's easy, but because you've decided you're worth staying with.

You've just explored resilience — the quiet, steady ability to reset, adjust, and keep going no matter what the match or life throws at you. Resilience keeps you in the fight. Resilience keeps you grounded. Resilience keeps you moving forward.

But resilience alone doesn't guarantee clarity. There are moments — in tennis and in life — where the pressure spikes, the emotions rise, the stakes feel heavy, and the mind starts to wobble. Moments where resilience keeps you standing, but composure determines how you stand. Because the truth is this: You can be resilient and still play tight. You can be resilient and still panic. You can be resilient and still lose yourself in the moment. Composure is what keeps your mind steady when the world around you isn't.

So now we shift from resilience to composure — the skill that allows you to stay centered under pressure.

CHAPTER 19

Composure

***

Staying Centered When the Moment Gets Loud

Composure is one of the most underrated skills in tennis. People think it means staying calm. People think it means not caring. People think it means being emotionless. But composure isn't the absence of emotion — it's the ability to stay grounded inside emotion.

There's a moment in every match when the air changes. You feel it before you can explain it — a tightening in your chest, a quickening in your breath, a sudden awareness that the moment has grown bigger than the point you're playing. Maybe the score is close. Maybe the crowd gets louder. Maybe your mind starts racing ahead, imagining outcomes that haven't happened yet. Composure begins right there, in that fragile space between what you feel and what you choose to do next.

People often imagine composure as a kind of emotional stillness, like the great players don't feel anything at all. But that's a myth. Everyone feels the pressure. Everyone feels the nerves. Everyone feels the moment tugging at them.

Composure isn't the absence of emotion — it's the ability to stay connected to yourself while the emotion moves through you. Sometimes composure looks like a long breath that settles your shoulders. Sometimes it's the decision to slow your walk to the baseline. Sometimes it's the quiet reminder that you're still here, still capable, still in the match. It's subtle, almost invisible from the outside. But inside, it's a reclaiming — a return to yourself.

Your body is usually the first thing to betray you. Before your mind admits you're rattled, your grip tightens, your swing stiffens, your vision narrows. You start rushing without realizing it. The body speaks before the mind does. And the body also knows how to guide you back. A deeper exhale. A softer jaw. A slower tempo. These small physical shifts aren't techniques — they're invitations back into the moment.

The real battle for composure happens in the mind. Not in the thoughts themselves, but in your relationship to them. Pressure magnifies everything — your fears, your stories, your expectations. Suddenly a simple point feels like a referendum on your identity. You start imagining what happens if you lose. You replay the mistake you just made. You judge yourself for feeling nervous in the first place.

Composure is the ability to notice all of that without getting swept away. It's the quiet acknowledgment: "Yes, I'm nervous. Yes, this moment matters. And yes, I'm still capable of playing this point." Neutrality isn't coldness — it's honesty without panic. Big moments don't require big emotions. They require big clarity. And clarity only shows up when you're willing to slow down enough to see the moment for what it is — not what your fear says it is. When you're composed, the court feels bigger again. Your swing loosens. Your decisions sharpen. You stop reacting and start responding.

Composure isn't something you turn on for the important points. It's something you build in the quiet ones. It's built in the way you breathe after a mistake, the way you talk to yourself when you're frustrated, the way you choose presence over panic when the match starts to tilt. It's built in the small, unglamorous moments where you decide not to abandon yourself.

Life tests your composure just as relentlessly as tennis does. A difficult conversation. A stressful day. A moment where everything feels uncertain. Composure in life isn't about being stoic — it's about staying steady enough to choose your next step with intention instead of fear. It's emotional maturity in motion.

Composure isn't perfection. It's connection — to your breath, to your body, to your intention, to the part of you that knows how to navigate the moment even when the moment feels overwhelming.

"It's the quiet strength of staying with yourself when everything else tries to pull you away."

You've just explored composure — the ability to stay centered when the moment gets loud, when emotions rise, and when pressure tries to pull you out of yourself. Composure is the skill that keeps you grounded. It's the skill that keeps you steady. It's the skill that keeps you connected.

But composure alone doesn't create confidence. Confidence isn't built in the easy moments. Confidence isn't built when everything is going your way. Confidence isn't built when you're winning comfortably. Confidence is built when you stay composed long enough to see that you can handle the moment.

Confidence is the natural outcome of:

- Presence
- Acceptance
- Letting go
- Self-trust
- Resilience

- Composure

Confidence is what rises when you stop abandoning yourself.

So now we shift from composure to confidence — the deep, internal kind that doesn't depend on the scoreboard.

CHAPTER 20

Confidence

***

The Quiet Belief That You Can Handle the Moment

Confidence is rarely what tennis players imagine it to be. People think it's loud. People think it's hype. People think it's swagger. People think it's something you "feel" before you play well. The truth is that real confidence is none of those things. Real confidence is quiet and steady. Real confidence is earned and it is internal. Confidence isn't the belief that you'll win — it's the belief that you can handle whatever happens.

Confidence has a reputation it doesn't deserve. People talk about it like it's a mood you wake up with, or a personality trait some players are born having. But real confidence is quieter than that, steadier than that, and far more earned than people realize. It's not lightning. It's sediment — something that builds layer by layer through experience, resilience, trust, presence, and the simple act of recovering again and again.

Confidence is the belief that you can handle yourself. Not perfectly. Not effortlessly. Just honestly. It's the belief that you can adjust when the match shifts, compete when things get uncomfortable, stay present when your mind wants to run, and recover when the moment knocks you off balance. Confidence is self-trust in motion.

There's a kind of confidence that looks strong but collapses quickly — the kind that depends on winning, on playing well, on feeling good, on everything going your way. That version is fragile. It disappears the moment the match stops cooperating. And then there's the deeper kind — the kind that comes from who you are rather than what's happening. The kind that shows up in how you respond, how you compete, how you handle adversity. This confidence doesn't vanish when the match gets messy. It stays with you because it's built on identity, not outcome.

Confidence grows in small, almost forgettable moments. The quiet repetition of hitting your targets. The discipline of sticking to your patterns. The decision to stay present instead of spiraling. The ability to recover quickly instead of carrying mistakes with you. These small wins stack up. They build belief from the inside out.

Recovery plays a huge role in confidence. Every time you bounce back from a mistake, you reinforce the message: I can handle this. Consistency matters too — not perfection, but stability. And courage is part of the equation. Confidence doesn't grow when you avoid risk. It grows when you step into it, when you take action even when you're unsure. But confidence can break — and it usually breaks in predictable ways. It cracks when you chase perfection, when you judge yourself harshly, when you tie your identity to results, when you panic after mistakes, when you abandon your patterns, when you overthink, when you try to control everything. Confidence breaks the moment you stop trusting yourself.

Always remember, pressure doesn't destroy confidence. It reveals it. Under pressure, the players who trust themselves don't get louder — they get calmer. Their confidence isn't a performance. It's a presence.

Similarly, life asks for confidence just as much as tennis does. Confidence in life is trusting your decisions, speaking honestly, taking risks, setting boundaries, showing up as yourself, choosing growth over comfort. It's the belief that you can navigate the unknown — not because you know what will happen, but because you know who you are.

If you've lost confidence, that's not a failure. It's a sign that you've lived. It's a sign that you've tried. Confidence can always be rebuilt. You rebuild it by returning to your routines, simplifying your decisions, stacking small wins, practicing presence, accepting what is, letting go of what isn't yours to carry, and rebuilding trust with yourself one moment at a time.

Remember, confidence isn't about believing you'll win. It's about believing you can handle whatever the moment brings. It's the belief that you can adjust, recover, stay present, stay composed, stay connected, stay yourself.

You've just explored confidence — the deep, internal belief that you can handle the moment, no matter what the moment brings. Confidence is the quiet strength that grows from presence, trust, resilience, and composure.

But confidence alone doesn't move you forward. Confidence tells you — you can. Courage is what makes you do it. Confidence is belief. Courage is action. Confidence is internal. Courage is expressed. Confidence is the foundation. Courage is the leap.

So now we shift from confidence to courage — the skill that turns all your inner work into outward movement.

CHAPTER 21

COURAGE

***

THE WILLINGNESS TO ACT, EVEN WHEN YOU'RE AFRAID

Courage is a concept that is often misrepresented in tennis and in life. People think courage means fearlessness. People think courage means aggression. People think courage means taking wild risks. But real courage is quieter than that.

Courage in tennis rarely looks like the highlight reel moments people imagine. It's almost never the screaming winner at 5-all in the third or the chest-pounding celebration after a big point. Real courage is quieter. It happens in the small, private decisions a player makes long before the crowd notices anything.

Courage is choosing intention over fear when you're standing on the baseline at break point down, knowing the safe play is to guide the ball — and choosing instead to hit the forehand you've trained a thousand times. It's choosing presence over panic when your mind starts sprinting ahead to what happens if you lose the next two points. It's choosing honesty over comfort when you admit to yourself that you're nervous, instead of pretending you're not. It's choosing growth over safety when you go after your second serve instead of rolling it in and hoping for the best. It's choosing action even when doubt is loud.

"Courage isn't the absence of fear. It's the decision to move anyway."

Players often think courage is something you're born with — a personality trait reserved for the bold, the fearless, the naturally confident. But courage is a choice, not a gift. It's the willingness to swing freely under pressure, to take the right risks, to trust your patterns when everything in you wants to abandon them, to stay present when fear rises, to compete honestly, to show up as yourself even when the moment feels too big.

"Courage is the bridge between who you are and who you're becoming."

Fear is part of the game. Every player carries it. Fear of missing. Fear of losing. Fear of being judged. Fear of disappointing people. Fear of not being enough. You see it in the way a player tightens their grip on a big point, or in the way they start aiming for the middle of the court when the scoreboard gets close. Fear isn't the problem — the story attached to it is.

- Fear says, "If you miss, it means something about you."
- Fear says, "If you lose, people will judge you."
- Fear says, "If you fail, you'll look weak."

Courage rewrites the story. Courage says, "Misses don't define me." Courage says, "Losing doesn't diminish me." Courage says, "Failure is part of growth."

You see courage most clearly in the big moments — the tight score lines, the heavy stakes, the points where your heartbeat feels louder than the crowd. Courage is the player who sticks to their patterns at 30-40 instead of panicking into a bailout shot. It's the player who trusts their swing on a second serve instead of guiding it. It's the player who stays present instead of spiraling into what-ifs. It's the player who keeps their identity intact when the moment tries to pull it apart.

However, the courage that actually changes a player's career — and their life — is much smaller. It's micro-courage. The kind that happens in the quiet moments no one sees. The breath you take before reacting. The decision to choose a target instead of panicking. The willingness to stick to your patterns after a mistake instead of abandoning them. The honesty to admit when you're scared. The resilience to try again after failure. The presence to stay with yourself when your mind wants to run.

"Micro-courage builds macro-change."

Life itself demands courage just as much as tennis does. Courage in life is having the difficult conversation you've been avoiding. It's taking a risk that matters. It's leaving a situation that no longer serves you. It's starting something new. It's letting yourself be seen. It's telling the truth. It's being yourself even when it feels easier to shrink.

Courage grows through action, not thought. You don't think your way into courage — you act your way into it. Every time you choose presence over panic, honesty over avoidance, intention over fear, you strengthen the muscle. Every time you take a small risk, you build a little more trust in yourself. Every time you move toward the moment instead of away from it, you become a little more courageous.

Courage is the moment you choose yourself — especially when fear tells you not to.

You've just explored courage — the willingness to act even when fear is present, the willingness to swing freely under pressure, the willingness to choose growth over comfort. Courage is what moves you forward. Courage is what breaks patterns. Courage is what opens doors.

Courage alone isn't sustainable. Courage helps you take the first step. Patience helps you take the next thousand.

The truth is this: "Growth doesn't happen at the speed of courage — it happens at the speed of patience."

So now we shift from courage to patience — the skill that allows you to stay committed, stay grounded, and stay steady through the long, slow, beautiful process of becoming who you're meant to be.

CHAPTER 22

PATIENCE

***

THE DISCIPLINE TO LET GROWTH UNFOLD AT ITS OWN PACE

Patience is the skill most players overlook until it's too late. People think patience is passive. People think patience is waiting. People think patience is doing nothing. The real patience is active, disciplined and intentional.

Patience is the ability to:

- Stay committed when progress is slow
- Stay grounded when emotions rise
- Stay focused when results don't show up
- Stay steady when doubt creeps in
- Stay present when the future feels far away

"Patience is the long game."

1. **What Patience Really Is**
    - Patience isn't about slowing down — it's about not rushing.
    - Patience isn't about waiting — it's about trusting.
    - Patience isn't about doing less — it's about doing the right things consistently.

   Patience is the belief that:

    - Growth takes time
    - Mastery takes repetition

- Confidence takes experience
- Resilience takes practice
- Breakthroughs take persistence

Patience is the discipline to stay the course.

2. Patience on the Court

Tennis demands patience in every dimension.

A. *Patience in Points*

- Not forcing winners.
- Not panicking when rallies get long.
- Not rushing your patterns.

B. *Patience in Matches*

- Not collapsing after a slow start.
- Not giving up when momentum shifts.
- Not expecting perfection.

C. *Patience in Development*

- Not expecting instant improvement.
- Not judging yourself too quickly.
- Not abandoning your process.

Patience is the ability to let the game unfold without trying to control every moment.

3. The Impatience Spiral

Impatience is one of the biggest killers of performance. Impatience sounds like:

- "Why am I not playing better?"
- "This should be easier."
- "I should be further along."
- "I can't believe I'm still making this mistake."

Impatience creates:

- Tension
- Frustration
- Rushed decisions
- Emotional spirals
- Self-judgment

Impatience pulls you out of the moment. Patience brings you back.

4. Patience in Life

Life demands patience just as much as tennis does.

Life patience looks like:

- Trusting your growth
- Allowing relationships to evolve
- Giving yourself time to heal
- Letting your career unfold
- Accepting that progress isn't linear
- Choosing consistency over urgency

"Always remember, we build patience through practice — not perfection."

You don't become great by rushing. You become great by staying for the long game. Patience is the game that builds champions — on the court and in life.

You've just explored patience — the discipline to let growth unfold at its own pace, the maturity to stay committed even when progress is slow, the steadiness to trust the long game. Patience keeps you grounded. Patience keeps you steady. Patience keeps you from rushing the process but patience alone doesn't create progress.

Patience is the mindset where discipline is the action. Patience helps you stay calm while discipline helps you stay consistent.

Remember: You don't rise to the level of your motivation — you rise to the level of your discipline.

So now we shift from patience to discipline — the skill that turns intention into reality.

CHAPTER 23

DISCIPLINE

***

THE CONSISTENCY THAT TURNS GROWTH INTO A HABIT

Discipline doesn't announce itself. It doesn't feel dramatic or heroic. Most of the time, it feels like nothing at all — just a quiet decision you make when no one is watching. People imagine discipline as intensity, as grinding, as pushing yourself to the edge. But real discipline is far less glamorous. It's clarity. It's alignment. It's self-respect expressed through action.

If you watch a disciplined player closely, you won't see anything flashy. You'll see someone tying their shoes the same way every day. You'll see someone warming up with intention instead of going through the motions. You'll see someone choosing the right shot even when the wrong one is more tempting. You'll see someone who doesn't need the match to be perfect in order to stay connected to themselves.

Discipline is the quiet agreement you make with yourself about who you're becoming — and then honoring that agreement in the smallest moments. On the court, discipline shows up long before the scoreboard does. It's in the way you move your feet on a ball you don't feel like chasing. It's in the way you breathe after a mistake instead of letting frustration take over. It's in the way you return to your patterns when the match gets messy. It's in the way you choose intention over impulse, clarity over chaos, steadiness over panic. A disciplined player doesn't rely on motivation. Motivation is a spark — discipline is the structure that keeps the fire burning.

Emotional discipline is its own kind of strength. It's not about shutting down your feelings. It's about directing them. It's the moment you feel frustration rising and choose to breathe instead of react. It's the moment you feel doubt creeping in and choose to stay with your routines. It's the moment the match gets loud and you decide to stay steady instead of getting swept away.

Routines are where discipline becomes visible. They're not rigid — they're stabilizing. They give you rhythm when the match feels chaotic. They give you grounding when your emotions start to wobble. They give you clarity when your mind wants to sprint ahead. A strong routine doesn't limit you — it frees you. It gives you something to return to when everything else feels uncertain.

However, discipline doesn't stop at the baseline. Life demands it just as much as tennis does. Discipline in life is keeping promises to yourself even when it's inconvenient. It's choosing long-term growth over short-term comfort. It's setting boundaries that protect your energy. It's showing up for your goals on the days you'd rather hide from them. It's doing the small things well — not because anyone is watching, but because you've decided that's who you are.

Discipline doesn't feel like a breakthrough. It feels like consistency. It feels like steadiness. It feels like choosing the next right action even when no one will ever know. And over time, those small choices accumulate into something powerful — a version of yourself you can trust.

You've just explored discipline — the steady, self-aligned consistency that turns growth into a habit. Discipline is what keeps you showing up. Discipline is what keeps you grounded. Discipline is what keeps you aligned with the player and person you want to become.

Discipline alone doesn't guarantee clarity.

You can show up every day ...
You can do the work ...
You can follow your routines ...
You can stay committed ...
... but if your attention is scattered, your performance will be too.

Remember this: Your mind is always focusing on something — the question is whether it's focusing on the right thing.

So now we shift from discipline to focus — the skill that directs your energy, your intention, and your presence toward what actually matters.

CHAPTER 24

Focus

***

Directing Your Attention Toward What Matters Most

Focus is far more than just keeping your eye on the ball. People imagine it as a kind of tunnel vision — a narrowing of the world until only the ball exists. But real focus is nothing like that. Real focus is spacious. It's flexible. It's selective. It's the ability to place your attention where it helps you and pull it away from where it hurts you.

If you've ever watched a great player up close, you'll notice something subtle: Their attention moves. It doesn't lock. It shifts with the moment. Before the point, their eyes soften. Between points, their breath deepens. As the rally begins, their awareness widens to take in the court, the opponent, the ball. And then, when the moment demands it, their attention narrows just enough to make a clean decision.

Focus isn't stillness. It's navigation.

On the court, focus is the quiet ability to choose what matters. Sometimes that means noticing the height of the incoming ball. Sometimes it means feeling the tension in your shoulders. Sometimes it means recognizing that the momentum has shifted and adjusting your patterns.

Focus is the bridge between your intention and your execution — the thing that keeps you connected to the match instead of drifting into the stories your mind wants to tell. And those stories can be loud.

Focus breaks long before a player realizes it. It breaks when frustration hijacks your attention. It breaks when fear pulls you into the future. It breaks when ego starts arguing with the moment. It breaks when perfectionism whispers that anything less than flawless is failure. It breaks when comparison steals your presence. It breaks when you start replaying the last mistake instead of preparing for the next ball. Broken focus feels like your mind scattering in a dozen directions at once. You're on the court, but you're not really here.

Restoring focus isn't about forcing your mind to behave. It's about returning to yourself. Sometimes that return begins with a single breath — the kind that drops your shoulders and widens your awareness. Sometimes it's the feeling of your feet grounding into the court. Sometimes it's the softening of your eyes. Sometimes it's choosing a simple target. Sometimes it's the quiet repetition of a phrase that brings you back: one point, trust it, breathe.

Under pressure, focus becomes even more essential. Pressure tries to scatter your attention — to pull you into the future, into the outcome, into the fear of what might happen. Presence gathers it. The players who handle pressure well aren't necessarily calmer; they're simply better at returning to what matters. Their breath slows. Their movements smooth out. Their decisions simplify. They stay connected to their patterns instead of getting lost in the moment's noise.

"Focus is the difference between reacting and responding."

Focus in life is choosing your priorities instead of letting distractions choose them for you. It's directing your energy intentionally. It's staying present in conversations instead of drifting into your own thoughts. It's giving your attention to what matters and letting go of what doesn't. It's living with intention instead of autopilot.

CHAPTER 25

INTENTION

***

THE DIRECTION BEHIND EVERY THOUGHT, MOVEMENT, AND DECISION

Intention is the invisible force that separates a purposeful game from a reactive one. People talk about it like it's a plan, a goal, a wish for how things might go. But intention isn't something you hope for — it's something you choose. It's the quiet decision you make before the point begins, the decision that shapes how you move, how you think, how you respond.

"Intention is the why behind the what. It's the reason your game has direction instead of drift."

On the court, intention is always present — the question is whether you're choosing it or letting the moment choose for you. A player without intention gets pulled around by the match. They react instead of respond. They hit instead of choose. They chase instead of direct. They panic instead of adjust. They play whatever moment they're given instead of shaping the one they want.

A player with intention moves differently. There's a steadiness to them, a sense of direction that doesn't depend on the score. They pick a target. They pick a pattern. They pick a tempo. They pick a mindset. They pick a purpose. Their game has structure because their attention has structure.

Intention isn't just tactical — it's layered. There's the intention behind the shot you're hitting, the intention behind the thoughts you're choosing, and the intention behind the way you want to feel in the moment. Great players align all three. They know what they're trying to do with the ball. They know how they want to think. They know how they want to feel. Their game becomes coherent — not because the match is easy, but because they're anchored in something deeper than the score.

Intention, however, could also be fragile. It breaks the moment your attention gets hijacked. Fear pulls you into the future. Frustration drags you into the past. Ego tries to protect you. Perfectionism tightens your grip. Comparison steals your presence. Overthinking scatters your mind. Intention dissolves the moment you stop choosing it.

The good news is that intention returns the moment you choose it again. Sometimes it's a breath — the kind that drops your shoulders and clears the noise. Sometimes it's the feeling of your feet grounding into the court. Sometimes it's the decision to pick a simple target. Sometimes it's a quiet phrase that brings you back: one point, trust it, commit. Intention doesn't require perfect conditions. It requires a decision.

Under pressure, intention becomes even more essential. Pressure tries to scatter your mind, to pull you into the outcome, to make you forget who you are. Intention gathers you. It simplifies you. It steadies you. The players who handle pressure well aren't the ones who feel less — they're the ones who return to their intention faster. They commit. They breathe. They trust. They stay present. They stay connected.

Intention doesn't end at the baseline. Life demands it just as much as tennis does. Intention in life is choosing how you want to show up. It's directing your energy toward what matters. It's aligning your actions with your values. It's living with purpose instead of autopilot. It's making decisions that reflect who you want to become, not who you're afraid of being. Intention is how you stay connected to yourself when the world tries to pull you away.

You've just explored intention — the clarity and purpose behind every action, every decision, every point, every moment. Intention gives your game direction. Intention gives your presence meaning. Intention gives your awareness a target.

It's important to remember that intention alone doesn't create transformation.

You can know what you want ...

You can know why it matters ...

You can know how you want to show up ...

You can know the direction you want to move ...

... but without commitment, intention fades the moment things get uncomfortable.

"Intention sets the direction. Commitment keeps you on the path."

So now we shift from intention to commitment — the skill that makes growth inevitable.

CHAPTER 26

COMMITMENT

***

THE DECISION TO STAY WITH THE JOURNEY, EVEN WHEN IT'S HARD

Commitment isn't loud. It doesn't come with fireworks or adrenaline or the kind of motivation that makes you feel invincible for a day. Commitment is quieter than that — and far more durable. It's the long-term version of courage, the steady willingness to keep showing up long after the excitement fades.

Most players think commitment is intensity. They imagine it as a kind of relentless push, a constant grind, a refusal to rest. But real commitment isn't about force. It's about alignment. It's the decision to keep honoring the things that you say matter to you — your values, your routines, your process — even on the days when you don't feel like it.

On the court, commitment reveals itself in the smallest moments. It's the choice to stick to your patterns when fear tells you to bail out. It's trusting your targets when your mind wants to play it safe. It's staying present after a mistake instead of spiraling into frustration. It's breathing through pressure instead of tightening up. It's choosing clarity over panic, intention over impulse, honesty over shortcuts. Commitment is the decision to play your game — especially when the moment tries to pull you away from it.

You see commitment most clearly in the long rallies, the ones that test your patience more than your technique.

You see it in the way a player resets after an error, not with drama but with steadiness. You see it in the way they stay composed under pressure, not because they're fearless but because they've decided to stay connected to themselves. Commitment is the backbone of consistency — the thing that keeps your game from collapsing when the match gets messy.

Every player eventually hits what I call the commitment dip. It's the stretch where everything feels harder than it should. The progress slows. The excitement fades. The work feels repetitive. Doubt creeps in. Fatigue shows up. The emotional noise gets louder. This is where most players fall off — not because they lack talent, but because they lose commitment.

"The dip isn't a sign you're failing. The dip is a sign you're growing."

Commitment is deeply tied to identity. Players who know who they are commit more easily. They stay grounded under pressure. They stay aligned with their values. They stay connected to their purpose. Their commitment isn't something they force — it's something that flows naturally from the person they've decided to be.

Commitment in life is showing up for your goals even when progress is slow. It's honoring your values when it would be easier to abandon them. It's staying consistent with your habits when no one is watching. It's choosing growth over comfort, patience over urgency, truth over convenience. It's staying true to yourself when the world tries to pull you in a hundred different directions.

Commitment isn't built through intensity. It's built through repetition — the small, steady choices that accumulate over time. It grows when you clarify your values, simplify your routines, reduce friction, and create habits you can repeat on your worst days. It grows when you celebrate consistency instead of perfection. It grows when you forgive yourself quickly and return to your intention without drama. Commitment isn't a personality trait. It's a practice — one you renew every day.

You've just explored commitment — the deep, steady decision to stay with the journey, stay with your values, and stay with yourself even when the path gets hard. Commitment is what keeps you grounded. Commitment is what keeps you consistent. Commitment is what keeps you aligned, but commitment alone doesn't nourish you. Without gratitude, the journey becomes heavy. Gratitude is what reminds you why you started in first place.

Commitment keeps you on the path.
Gratitude makes the path worth walking.

So now we shift from commitment to gratitude — the skill that brings warmth, perspective, and emotional balance to the entire mental game.

CHAPTER 27

GRATITUDE

***

THE PERSPECTIVE THAT BRINGS LIGHTNESS, JOY, AND MEANING BACK INTO THE GAME

Gratitude has a way of softening the edges of the world. It doesn't erase difficulty or pretend everything is perfect. It simply reminds you that even in the middle of struggle, there is still something steady beneath your feet. Gratitude is grounding. It's stabilizing. It's energizing. It shifts your perspective just enough to let you breathe again.

Most players think gratitude is something you feel only when things are going well — when the shots land, when the body feels good, when the match is flowing. But real gratitude isn't tied to comfort. Real gratitude shows up when things are hard. It's the ability to recognize what's good even when the moment is heavy. It's clarity with warmth.

On the court, gratitude doesn't look dramatic. It's subtle. It's the quiet appreciation of the chance to compete. It's valuing the challenge in front of you instead of resenting it. It's respecting your opponent because they're the one pulling the best out of you. It's noticing your own growth, even if the scoreboard doesn't show it yet. It's enjoying the battle — not because it's easy, but because it matters to you.

Gratitude changes the way you experience pressure. Pressure narrows your world. It makes everything feel urgent, fragile, high-stakes. Gratitude widens it again. It reminds you that you're not trapped in the moment — you're participating in it.

When you're grateful, you breathe deeper. You see the court more clearly. You reconnect with your purpose. You release fear. You stay grounded. Gratitude becomes the antidote to panic. It also improves performance in ways players rarely expect. It reduces anxiety. It steadies your emotions. It sharpens your presence. It helps you make cleaner decisions. It strengthens resilience. It deepens enjoyment. Gratitude doesn't make you soft — it makes you steady. It brings you back to why you play in the first place.

In life, gratitude works the same way. It's appreciating the people who support you. It's valuing the opportunities you've earned. It's recognizing your growth even when it feels slow. It's noticing the small joys that would be easy to overlook. It's staying connected to what matters instead of getting lost in what doesn't. Gratitude makes life richer, deeper, more meaningful.

Lastly, gratitude doesn't ask you to ignore your struggles. It asks you to remember your strength. It doesn't ask you to pretend everything is easy. It asks you to stay connected to what's meaningful. Gratitude is the quiet reminder that even in the hardest moments, there is still something good here — something worth noticing, something worth valuing, something worth returning to.

You've just explored gratitude— the ability to appreciate the journey without being consumed by it. Gratitude brings balance and emotional maturity but gratitude alone doesn't complete the journey.

You can see the bigger picture ...
You can understand the moment ...
You can interpret your emotions ...
You can recognize your growth ...
You can stay grounded in your identity ...
... but there's one final step:
Integration.

Taking everything you've learned ...
everything you've practiced ...
everything you've discovered ...
everything you've unlearned ...
everything you've become ...
... and weaving it into the way you live, compete, think, and show up.

"Mental toughness isn't a collection of skills — it's a way of being."

So now we shift to the final chapter, the final transformation, the moment where the reader steps into the player and person they've been building toward.

CHAPTER 28

INTEGRATION

***

BECOMING THE PLAYER — AND PERSON — YOU WERE MEANT TO BE

There comes a point in the mental game where everything you've practiced stops feeling like separate pieces. Presence, trust, resilience, composure, confidence, courage, patience, discipline, focus, gratitude, intention, commitment — they stop living in their own chapters. They stop being skills you reach for. They stop being concepts you try to remember. They simply become you.

Integration is the moment the work you've done begins to weave itself together. It's not dramatic. It's not loud. It doesn't arrive with a breakthrough or a perfect match. Integration shows up quietly, almost without your noticing, in the way you move, the way you breathe, the way you respond to the moment. It's the shift from effort to expression.

Integration isn't perfection. It isn't mastery. It isn't control. Integration is alignment — the merging of who you are with how you play. It's the ability to live your values instead of just naming them. To trust your identity instead of searching for it. To stay connected to yourself instead of getting pulled into the noise. To respond instead of react. To choose instead of drift. To act with clarity. To compete with freedom.

When integration takes root, tennis feels different. You feel lighter, clearer, calmer. You feel grounded without being rigid. Intentional without being tense. Connected without being consumed. Your game becomes simpler, smoother, more instinctive. You're no longer fighting yourself. You're no longer chasing perfection. You're no longer trying to control every bounce, every swing, every outcome. You're simply playing — and playing from a deeper place.

Integration reveals itself most clearly in the tough moments. When momentum slips. When pressure rises. When frustration spikes. When doubt creeps in. When fatigue sets in. When the match feels bigger than you. These are the moments where the old version of you would tighten, panic, spiral, or disconnect. But the integrated version of you does something different.

You breathe and trust yourself. You stay here and remember you can handle this. You return to one point, one ball, one intention. Integration is the moment your training becomes your instinct.

Integration doesn't stop at the baseline. It's a life concept as much as a tennis one. It's living with intention instead of autopilot. Acting with clarity instead of confusion. Choosing with awareness instead of habit. Responding with composure instead of reactivity. Trusting your values instead of chasing approval. Staying grounded in who you are instead of who you think you should be.

"Integration is the moment your inner world and outer world match."

Just like everything meaningful, integration is a process. It grows through repetition, reflection, awareness, honesty, patience, presence, and self-trust. It grows quietly, gradually, naturally — not when you force it, but when you allow it. Not when you chase it, but when you live it. Integration is the final step in the mental game — and the beginning of everything that comes next.

EPILOGUE

You Are Ready

***

If you've made it to this point, you've done something most players never do — you've looked inward. You've explored the parts of the game that don't show up on scoreboards or highlight reels. You've stepped into the deeper work. The real work. The work that lasts.

And that matters.

Because tennis isn't just a sport. It's a mirror. It reflects your habits, your fears, your patterns, your strengths, your stories, your identity. It reveals who you are — and who you're becoming.

This book wasn't written to make you perfect. It was written to make you aware. To make you present. To make you connected. To make you yourself.

You've learned how to:

- Trust yourself
- Accept the moment
- Let go
- Stay present
- Find flow
- Build resilience
- Stay composed
- Cultivate confidence
- Act with courage
- Practice patience
- Live with discipline

- Direct your focus
- Choose intention
- Honor commitment
- Feel gratitude
- Integrate everything

These aren't just mental skills — they're ways of being. They're the foundation of a life lived with clarity, purpose, and authenticity.

And here's the truth: You already have everything you need. You always did. This book just helped you see it. The mental game isn't about becoming someone new. It's about removing the noise that keeps you from being who you already are.

You are capable.
You are resilient.
You are adaptable.
You are grounded.
You are enough.
You are ready.

Not because you've mastered every skill.
Not because you'll never struggle again.
Not because you'll never feel fear or doubt.

You're ready because you now know how to meet those moments with presence, honesty, and intention.

You're ready because you've built a relationship with yourself that won't collapse under pressure.

You're ready because you've learned how to stay connected — to your breath, your body, your values, your identity.

You're ready because you've learned how to *return to yourself*.

And that's the real victory.

AUTHOR'S NOTE

***

From Me to You

I didn't write this book because I had everything figured out.
I wrote it because I've lived every chapter in here — on the court, off the court, in the quiet moments, and in the messy ones.

I've felt the pressure.
I've felt the doubt.
I've felt the frustration of wanting to be better faster.
I've felt the weight of expectations —
my own and everyone else's.
I've felt the sting of setbacks and the slow burn of growth.

And I've also felt the joy.

The freedom.
The clarity.
The moments where everything clicks.
The moments where the game feels like an extension of who you are.
The moments where you surprise yourself.
The moments where you feel alive.

This book is a reflection of all of that —
the full spectrum.

It's built from years of playing, coaching, teaching, failing, learning, and watching players grow in ways that had nothing to do with their forehands or backhands. It's built from conversations on benches, in hallways, on practice courts, and during long walks after tough matches. It's built from the belief that the mental game isn't a luxury — it's the foundation.

And it's built from the truth I've seen over and over again: You are capable of more than you think — not because you're perfect, but because you're human.

If there's one thing I hope you take from this book, it's this:

You don't have to earn your worth.
You don't have to prove yourself to yourself.
You don't have to fight your way into confidence.
You don't have to perform your way into identity.

You just have to *return to yourself* —
again and again.
The mental game isn't about becoming someone new.
It's about uncovering who you've been all along.

So wherever you are in your journey —
early, late, stuck, rising, rebuilding, or reinventing —
I hope these pages help you feel a little more grounded, a little more connected, and a little more free.
And if you ever forget everything in this book, remember this one thing:

You can handle the moment.
You always have.
You always will.

Thank you for reading.
Thank you for growing.
Thank you for showing up —
not just to the court,
but to yourself.

— *Coach Emil*

RETURN to YOURSELF

The Mental Game of Tennis and Life

WORKSHEETS

***

Purpose:

*To step back, zoom out,
and notice how you're approaching the key areas of your life — what's working, what isn't,
and where you might be ready for a "second serve"
with a better strategy.*

How to use this:

- **Scan the QR Code** -or- **Take a Picture** and copy the URL into your web browser.
- **Take Your Time**. *Be honest, not harsh.*
- You're not grading yourself — you're getting information. Use extra space or journal if you need it.

What's inside:

- Worksheet 1: *Life Strategy Check-In*
- Worksheet 2: *Second Serve Planning*
- Worksheet 3: *Life as a Match — Daily/Weekly Journal*

DOWNLOAD YOUR
WORKSHEETS | BONUS | FREE

https://www.northernvatennis.com/worksheets

ACKNOWLEDGMENTS

***

The people who shaped this journey. No one grows alone — not in tennis, not in life, not in writing a book like this.

To the players I've coached over the years: Thank you for your honesty, your effort, your vulnerability, and your trust. You taught me more about the mental game than any textbook ever could. Every chapter in this book carries pieces of our conversations, our breakthroughs, and our shared moments on court.

To the mentors and coaches who shaped my understanding of the game: Your wisdom, your patience, and your belief in me built the foundation for everything I teach today. I'm grateful for every lesson — especially the ones I didn't understand until years later.

To the people in my life who supported me through the writing process: Thank you for the encouragement, the grounding, the perspective, and the space to create. Your presence made this possible.

To the reader holding this book: Thank you for giving your time, your attention, and your heart to this journey. Thank you for being willing to grow. Thank you for choosing to look inward. I hope these pages help you feel more connected to yourself — on the court and beyond it.

This book wouldn't have been possible without the help and guidance from Eli 'The Book Guy' Blyden. Thank you for taking a chance on me!

And finally, to the game of tennis itself: Thank you for being the greatest teacher I've ever had.

ABOUT THE AUTHOR

Emil Vassilev, (M.S. in Leadership), is a well-recognized and respected tennis coach. With an outstanding background as a former Division 1 collegiate tennis player, coach and a tour player in addition to many years of teaching experience, Emil brings both his passion and expertise to the court, helping you believe and achieve!

In 2016, Emil founded the "Emil Tennis Method©" which is a research-based, tennis movement and footwork training program. It allows the player to learn better and faster by applying actual tennis movement patterns in their game. Some of Coach Emil's credentials include being a current ATP Certified International Coach member of the GPTCA as well as a Certified Tennis Performance Trainer (TPT) by the International Tennis Performance Association (iTPA). In addition

Emil is a Certified USTA Coaching Professional and USTA Sports Science Level 1 certified.

Mr. Vassilev has been selected to serve as a USTA Spring Team National Coach for several years now. The USTA Spring Team Nationals is the highest-level junior team competition in the United States and only a handful of coaches are invited every year by the USTA, making it a very competitive selection process. In 2025 Coach Emil led his team the "Seahawks" to a national title!

Coach Emil's team won the 2025 Brewer Cup (USTA Spring Team Nationals) held in Mobile, AL.

2025 Brewer Cup USTA National Team Champions

OTHER BOOK BY EMIL

A Valuable Resource for Coaches & Players Alike...

- Mark Kovacs, PhD, CTPS, MTPS

Footwork is The Foundation for A Proper Shot!!!

- Andres Gomez: 1990 French Open Singles Champion & Former World Number 4 in Singles & Former World Number 1 in Doubles

Connect with Emil

If you would like to connect with Emil, please follow him on the following social media accounts:

Facebook: **@emiltennismethod**

Instagram: **@emiltennismethod**

* * *

WEBSITE:

www.NorthernVaTennis.com

* * *

For enquiries, please email:

info@NorthernVATennis.com

* * *

WORKSHEETS | BONUS | FREE

https://www.northernvatennis.com/worksheets

www.usta.com/tennis-coaches/emil-vassilev-2010711611

www.ingramcontent.com/pod-product-compliance
Lightning Source LLC
LaVergne TN
LVHW050650100826
845148LV00011B/2056

* 9 7 9 8 2 3 4 0 6 7 9 9 9 *